X-*TENDING*

Laura Laforce

Laura Laforce

Manor House

Library and Archives Canada Cataloguing in Publication

Laforce, Laura, 1966-, author
    X-tending / Laura Laforce.

ISBN 978-1-897453-38-4 (pbk.)

    1. Laforce, Laura, 1966-. 2. Psychics--Canada--
Biography. 3. Mediums--Canada--Biography. I. Title.
II. Title: Extending.

BF1027.L34A3 2013a   133.8092   C2013-902756-4

Published 2013: Manor House Publishing Inc.,
452 Cottingham Crescent, Ancaster, ON, Canada, L9G 3V6
905-648-2193 wwww.manor-house.biz All rights reserved
Cover Design/creation: Donovan Davie
Front cover art: Shutterstock / Bruce Rolff

We acknowledge the financial support of the Government of
Canada through the Canada Book Fund (CBF) for our
publishing activities.

Dedication

Early one morning, my dear friend Minnie went to Heaven. Even though death has happened, she isn't far away.

I knew she was leaving. I didn't have a say. Our connection remains as strong as it was yesterday.

You're a fine lovely angel and still my best friend. Even though you've left your earthshell, this definitely isn't the end.

> Minnie, I dedicate my book
> 'X-TENDING' to you.
> I love you always and forever,
> Your best friend,
>   Laura

CONTENTS

Introduction

A new awareness is upon us. People are forced out of their comfort zones. Millions struggle with challenges and diversity. The wool is pulled over their eyes and the carpets from beneath their feet. What they believed in yesterday is no longer concrete. Their governments are corrupt and their money is worthless. The faiths no longer have a stronghold, which previously provided comfort. Society has become negative, disconnected, and extremely dysfunctional. It's almost as if something opened Hell's nasty gate.

Earth is a distracting obstacle course full of endless challenges. This is the plane where our souls develop by encountering life. We pre-plan our lives before we arrive and déjà vu verifies this pre-existing knowledge. The hardships we experience are unfortunate, but necessary, in order to learn and understand.

Our world is not ending. Souls of the living are awakening in order to survive. The veil between the living and the dead is being lifted and valuable information is being sent from beyond. People are learning to reconnect through the simplicity of love. Loving people have healthy boundaries, where hurt doesn't serve a purpose.

Acknowledgements:

My thanks to Manor House Publishing,
my friends and family and all others
who believe in me

Books by Laura Laforce

Psychic Sight; X-tending; Journey into Spirituality; Finding X.

Website: www.lauralaforce.com

AUDIO CD

Guided Spiritual Meditation

Chapter One

Terrorism Exposed

Staring at the endless paperwork heaped on my desk, I sipped on my latte wishing away the mess. There was a column to write. A stack of fan mail sat unanswered. Loose papers needed filing, when a vision of heavy gold handcuffs suddenly appeared. Huge golden links embraced my right wrist. The other cuff remained open, lying on my desk. I couldn't see myself in trouble. I hadn't done anything wrong. I sat briefly wondering what this was about.

The energy accompanying these restraints was strangely liberating. It was as if someone was being set free. In the spirit world, gold is always good. Rather than jumping to conclusions, I chose to deal with my paperwork instead.

I grabbed the first piece of fan mail and started my reply. This is when an image of black capital solid letter "B" struck my third eye. This italicized font resembled those which spelled "B" as in Bin Laden in previous news headlines.

Another vision revealed a headless skeleton surrounded in fuchsia pink, indicating fury from the spiritual aspect. A missing skull represents the cause of death. This would mean the person had either been shot through the head or beheaded. I knew for a long time that he was still alive. I knew his death would be a sudden surprise.

I spent a few moments piecing together what I'd seen. I had recently seen a rash of eastern political deaths, including Bin Laden's, but never entertained them. Obviously this was extremely important, but I couldn't understand why.

I forced myself back into the reality of my paperwork. Within a couple of hours it was finally complete. I retreated to the living room with my husband TJ and switched on the television for a much needed break.

We were watching TV when the news of Osama Bin Laden's death hit. A speech from the balcony of the White House was being delivered. My ears started ringing loudly, diverting my attention. I shut my eyes to receive an urgent message coming in from beyond.

In an instant a similar, but much smaller balcony, was revealed. Thick black lines outlined the perimeter, reflecting danger. I opened my eyes and shut them again hoping this would stop. Again the same dire warning played out. This time the drawing included a tall slender tower in the distance. The drawing always started at the bottom left and ended in the upper right hand corner, resembling the old red Etch A Sketch boards with the two white knobs many of us played with as children.

Afterwards a dark number "6" hung in midair. The number was a time indicator. Did this refer to May sixth, six days, the month of June, six weeks or six months? I wasn't sure, but this wasn't good.

Explicit visions warned me of a looming terrorist attack in Washington DC. Visions of threatening drawings reflecting danger were repeatedly sent to me. I knew without a doubt an attack was being planned. Consequences would be deadly if the progression wasn't stopped. Drawn events can be prevented or altered, but they need to be somehow delivered.

"Spirit," I uttered in total desperation sitting at my desk.

"Please, don't show me this any more. I don't want to be involved. I don't know how to help. Send it to someone more capable." I closed my eyes again and the drawings immediately stopped.

The drawings resurfaced hours later on the living room wall. This time I spotted these with my open eyes.

"Laura," interrupted TJ with a concerned tone in his voice.

"What's going on? You seem to be disturbed. You're looking off in the distance. Aren't you interested in watching your favorite TV show?" TJ moved closer and sat directly beside me.

"I was trying to watch, but I keep seeing these horrible images being drawn on the wall. A terrorist attack is being planned in Washington DC. Lives will be lost, if this evil attack isn't stopped." I spoke in an upsetting tone trying to contain myself.

A wave of chills hit the both of us. Goosebumps and standing hairs plastered our forearms.

"What are you going to do about this?" TJ hesitantly asked, completely ignoring the TV.

"I'm not sure. I've contemplated calling the police, but I'm leery of them. The problem is they want concrete facts. I don't feel I have enough details. Not everyone is receptive to what I do. I don't know if they'll listen to some random Canadian." I sat beside TJ, leaning up against him.

"I sense you're very uneasy with this situation. I'm sure you'll find a way to deal with it. Remember when you used to complain about things being too soon and that you weren't ready yet. Your spirit guides are pushing you in a new direction." TJ tenderly reached over and squeezed my hand trying to reassure me.

"This one takes the cake, though. If I say something, I risk the chance of getting into lots of trouble. If I keep this to myself, many innocent people will end up dead." I sat fidgeting, unable to relax.

That night, I lay awake, unable to sleep. The disturbing images I had been shown kept running through my mind. While TJ slept, I sat on the edge of our bed contemplating what to do. An old fashioned black telephone popped before my eyes. Shortly before three o'clock in the morning, I climbed out of bed.

I rushed down the dark hallway into my cold office and flipped on the lights. Switching on the computer, I hunkered down in my squeaky leather chair. I ambitiously searched the web for law enforcement agencies in Washington DC. I needed to figure out which party to call. I'd never dealt with terrorism before. Three choices with numbers were displayed on my screen. These were: the Washington Police Department, FBI or the White House Police.

"Spirit, help me," I begged. The curser instantly moved by itself, lighting up the number that I needed to call. I quickly picked up the phone and dialed the number before I lost the courage.

"Washington Command Post," a tired male's soft voice answered.

"Is this the Washington Police Department?" I expected a high pitched rushed telephone operator, not a relaxed gentleman on the other end of the line.

"You've reached the command post. I'm the commander, what can I help you with?"

"I'm a psychic medium calling from Canada. I'm calling to warn you of a terrorist attack being planned in Washington DC." I paused, allowing the officer time to digest what I had said.

"What do you know about an upcoming terrorist attack?" The commander asked.

"I've been shown, through progressive drawings, the back balcony of the White House. There is a tall skinny tower about a football field away factored into the scene. Number six keeps being revealed after every frame." I tried desperately to catch my winded shaking breath.

"What importance does the number have?" The commander inquired, trying to piece together what I had told him.

"Six is a time line. This attack could happen on May sixth, but it could also happen in six weeks, the month of June or six months from now." I tried to help him understand by pointing out the other possibilities.

"You're saying this could happen four days from now? Is this correct?" The commander tried to search for confirmation.

"Yes, it could, but timelines are hard to figure out. All I know is when I see things they happen, unless they are stopped." I seriously hoped he'd be able to handle things himself after receiving this tip.

"Do you know who's behind this?" the pleasant commander asked.

"No, I haven't seen faces or names of those involved." I sat there hoping we were almost off the phone. I felt like I was in over my head.

"What about the method of attack?"

"A bull's eye appears in the centre of the White House's back yard. I would assume a bomb."

"Is there anything else you can tell me?"

"Not right now." Feeling under pressure, I was relieved that I hadn't been shown anything else.

"What do you mean by not right now?"

"Sometimes it takes days for visions to completely manifest. I often receive messages in segments instead of everything at once." I hoped he understood that I wasn't withholding anything.

"I understand some people have special gifts. I've rarely had an opportunity to speak with someone like you. Thank you for calling in. I'll pass this information along to the proper division."

Returning to bed, I accidentally woke up TJ. "How come you're up? Is everything okay?"

"Everything is taken care of. Let's go to sleep." I gently slid into bed beside him.

"What were you doing up?" TJ asked, rolling over in a daze.

"I was disturbed after seeing the terrorist attack, so I called the Washington Police," I briefly explained while pulling up my covers.

"You did what?" My loving husband was now fully awake. "You called Washington DC?" TJ's tone became excited and loud.

"Yes, I did."

"How did they react?" He lay beside me trying to cope with what I had just said. "I hope you didn't leave your name or number."

"It's a little too late, I already did."

"Oh my God," he freaked in total shock. "I don't know you. If this place is crawling with cops in the morning, I'll tell them I've never seen you before. I wished you'd just let things be. This isn't a minor crime you reported. You called in a national threat. You put Washington on alert. You put us at risk behaving this way."

"Life is full of risks. Living can be dangerous." I lay there silently regretting opening my big mouth.

"What are the neighbors going to think if our house is surrounded by the police cars?" TJ started squishing up his pillow. I lay there hoping he'd settle and go back to sleep.

"I guess that would be up to them. I haven't committed a crime. I'm trying to save lives of the innocent. Can't we just go to sleep?"

"I'm sorry Laura. I didn't expect you to call the police. I guess Spirit shows you these things, because you're not afraid to speak up."

TJ reached over and kissed me goodnight. I was on the verge of falling asleep when another image appeared. This time, a large elongated object moved in the dark. It moved very slowly and steadily around a curve. It appeared to be without wheels. The movement was unusual; almost vessel-like. This seemed to be only a short distance from the White House. I tried figure out what would move like that. It was too smooth for a limo and way too small for a cart. None of these seemed to fit. I couldn't see a street, but a dark open void, which usually indicates water. Out of exhaustion, I eventually fell asleep.

Morning came early. Being tired, I lazed around in bed while TJ got ready for work. This is when a black and white map lingered in front of my third eye. The map was drawn and labeled with abbreviations. The White House was labeled with a bull's eye. A solid black oval bomb resembling a grenade was displayed with a wick hanging out of the top. Several Capital "W's" were placed on various areas of the map. A couple of capital letters "M" and "J" were strategically placed." A street name was abbreviated "CN". Number "41" appeared at the very top. I grabbed a pen and paper and wrote everything down. This was going to be a challenge to decipher. I didn't know Washington. I had never been there.

Early that afternoon, I picked up my ringing phone.

"Hi, I'm an officer with the Washington Police Department," an authoritative voice boomed. "May I speak with Laura Laforce?"

"Speaking."

"I've been asked to touch base with you. I have a couple of questions to ask." Before he could continue my other line started to ring. It was another call from Washington. I let it ring through to my voicemail. Instantly I felt unsettled and tense. I kept my wits about me by reminding myself that these people were thousands of miles away and harmless. "I understand you called Washington Police Department in the middle of the night. Is that correct?"

"Yes."

"You spoke of being a psychic medium and of seeing a terrorist attack. You probably heard the news like the rest of the word that Osama Bin Laden is dead. Events like this tend to bring people like you out of the woodwork with illegitimate claims. They waste our time and dollars over their fantasies. I've never seen your name in our system before; perhaps you're legitimate. Past experience with crackpots tells me otherwise. Who did you get this information from?"

"I received the information from my spirit guides." "How do I know you're not attached to terrorists?"

"I'm not. I don't know who's involved. All I know is what I see."

"Which police department do you currently work for?"

"None, I'm not paid by any police department. I usually work through the victims, and on occasion I'll call the crime tips line."

Anxiety set in and my body started to tremble. I found this officer abrasive in the manner he was interrogating me. His attitude towards me was appallingly rude.

"Have you solved any cases?" "Several."

"Who are your official police references? I want names and numbers," he demanded.

"I'm on the road right now, but if you call me back in half an hour, I'll have some numbers for you."

"Police references?"

"No, personal references from prominent citizens." "Why don't you have police references?"

"I've never required any in the past. Officers I know personally would want to protect their interests." A severe tension headache started to intensely throb.

"Somebody else will be in contact with you shortly. Perhaps I'll contact you at some point later on. Good-bye."

I was relieved to hear his phone line disconnect. When I arrived home, I checked my voice mail. Another cop from the Suspicious Crimes Unit in Washington was waiting for me to return his call. I called TJ at work first, hoping to catch him at his desk. The first time around I was lucky.

"Guess what, TJ?"

"Are the cops buzzing around you?"

"No, but they've been on the phone. I regret calling the police last night. I just got off the phone with an abrasive, miserable, nasty cop who'd rather put me through the mill. He was skeptical and treated me like a bloody convict. If there's ever another time, I'll keep it to myself. He's upset me to the point that my head and stomach hurt. Another cop from the Suspicious Crimes Unit is waiting for me to return his call. It's hard to believe that helping can lead to being ridiculed. I feel like I'm in over my head."

"You need to talk to that other officer. Don't think about them all being bad. Perhaps they're playing good cop, bad cop with you. Sorry dear, but I've just been paged, I have to go."

I needed solid advice from someone in the industry. I called an acquaintance of mine, who happened to be an officer. I told him what was going on.

"Oh Laura, that's national security. They don't tread lightly on stuff like this. This is why these guys are behaving like brutes. Don't supply anyone's name for a reference. Act tough like me. Tell them they can take the information for what it is or leave it. I can't believe you informed them. Would it matter if a couple of hundred Americans lose their lives?" He addressed me in a condescending manner.

"Yes, it would." I couldn't comprehend why he'd ask such a question.

"Well, it shouldn't matter to you. Do you ever see anyone trying to save the Arabs? People are going to die. Whites and colored are sacrificed daily around the world.

Governments randomly dispose of people like chess pawns."

"I don't agree with you. These innocent people are individuals with souls. I wasn't referring to skin tones and ethnic groups. Perhaps you need to look deeper." I excused myself before gently hanging up the phone.

I made myself a cup of tea. Before returning the call I allowed my nerves to settle. I closed my eyes for a few minutes and connected with my guides. "Why is it that you guys give me the harder jobs? Wasn't there someone more capable of handling this than me?" A shining beam of light entered my line of vision; right away, I understood things would be all right. I grabbed the phone and called the officer who was patiently waiting.

"Hi, this is Laura Laforce. I'm returning your call."

"Hi Laura, I appreciate you calling me back." His tone was genuine and his energy was upbeat. "I understand you're gifted and that you've seen a terrorist attack?"

"Yes, I saw a terrorist attack drawn out."

"I understand you're a psychic. My roommate in college was that way. I envy people like you; unfortunately not all my colleagues feel the same."

Immediately I trusted this officer. I could share important information without it being censored. This person was capable of understanding and was willing to work with me.

"What did you see? Please take your time. Try to recall as much as possible."

"I received visions of an attack being planned in Washington. The small balcony on the back of the White House was repeatedly drawn out in black. This sketch includes a tall narrow tower off in the distance. The yard seems to be either a landmark or an area of intended target. To the west, a smooth vehicle sails through. I find this odd because it doesn't drive like a car or a truck. The number "41" is shown at the top of the map. The initials "CN" are possibly a nearby street. Five letter "W's" are displayed, representing names of buildings or objects. Two are straight west, another southwest, another appears at the very top of the map, probably representing Washington. One is laying sideways a couple of blocks northeast. A letter "J" is marked slightly above the west "W".

"How is the attack carried out?"

"Officer, I don't want to get into trouble using certain words, but may I, just this once?"

"Yes, go ahead."

"I see a ... bomb." I've always been taught to never use that word, especially around an airport or a cop.

"Thank you for sharing these details with me. I'm going to let you go. I need to go check out the areas and see what matches up. You mentioned it could happen in four days. I feel we should take time zones into consideration. What time is it where you are?

"Ten o'clock. Good, I'll be watching both time zones. Timing could be crucial. I'll call you back tomorrow morning."

Waking in the middle of the night, I saw the lit up vehicle previously revealed for a second time. This time it seemed to be floating around a bend. A building close by was labeled with the letter "J". The words **OCCULTS DIFFUSED** appeared in midair stacked on top of each other in white, puffy, large printing. Who were the occults? What did diffused mean? In the spiritual realm, white is a positive good color, but it was the message that I couldn't understand.

I went into the office and started up my computer, looking for possible definitions. In the quiet of the early morning hours, I could hear our bedroom door open, followed by the sound of TJ's footsteps.

"Good morning, my dear. I'm glad to see you're not calling Washington. May I ask what you're doing up in the middle of the night?"

"I'm trying to figure out the possible meaning of **OCCULTS DIFFUSED**, which Spirit spelled out to me in midair."

"Was it encrypted in black?"

"No, it was unusual. I've never seen a display like that in my entire life. The words were white, puffy and huge, which is a good sign, but I don't understand the meaning behind this."

"Do you need to understand everything you see?" "It sure makes things easier to handle."

"Why don't you come back to bed and sleep on it. Remember you have an important call in the morning and you need to be alert." TJ ushered me back to bed, knowing that I needed my rest.

In the morning, the constable called to touch base with me. "Hi Laura, you've totally blown me away. You're amazing; the things you mentioned completely match up. Constitution Avenue is the name of a nearby street. The alphabetical letters can be linked to buildings and restaurants. Did you see anything else?"

"I was shown the words **OCCULTS DIFFUSED** in white printing in midair, stacked on top of each other. I've never seen a presentation like this. I don't understand the meaning. In the dictionary, occults refer to some sort of eastern cells, and diffused means scattered. Obviously these two words hold major significance."

"Is there anything else?"

"My husband TJ has been searching the internet trying to match up things I've been shown, because we're unfamiliar with Washington. He found a ferry in the area. It resembles what I'd seen when it's lit up at night. This ferry travels around a bend; its movement is identical to what I'd seen in the vision of an unusual vessel. The JFK Building sits close to the shore."

"This makes sense. Remember, you couldn't understand what would move that way," the officer replied.

"My husband TJ mentioned to me earlier that the National Christmas Tree is in the back yard of the White House. There is an online photo of an interesting shadow generated on the ground from the peak of the tree, which resembles a bomb. Even though it looks similar, I still recalled seeing a bomb. Is this tree accessible to the public?"

"No, it's secured by a sixteen foot fence surrounding it."

"Are you absolutely sure nobody can get in or throw something over?"

"The area is fenced and guarded. Nobody is able to get in. I sure hope I'm on duty if something bad goes down."

I didn't want anything bad to happen to him. To me this man was amazing and selfless. He'd give his life to protect the citizens. I've never seen dedication like this in an officer.

"Can't you close off the area to the public?"

"No, we're not allowed to. This is a busy area, it would be impossible to shut down. Plus reacting like that would create public fear. We are watching and aware of the situation. We're doing our best to protect the people."

"Officer, please be careful. I wouldn't want you harmed."

"Laura, I want to be of service. I'm here for the people." Silence aired on both sides of the phone. I felt like crying. I didn't want this lovely man to put his life on the line, but this was his choice, not mine.

He told me he'd keep me in the loop, before hanging up our phones. "Spirit, if things get ugly over there, please spare this man."

Four days passed and nothing happened. I left a message on his phone: "Hi. It's Laura Laforce from Canada. Please keep watching these areas, I still sense danger. Things can still happen weeks and months later. Please be careful. Call me if you need anything."

Six good weeks were followed by an eventless June. The sensation of looming danger never ceased even though the drawings and messages did.

In late summer, a man did leap over the inaccessible sixteen foot fence that secures the White House. The man was taken into custody and later released. TJ and I wondered if this was a sequence of events before something major happened. We questioned if this was a setup by the terrorists to check out access to the yard. The media reported this man as being a protester. Was this trespasser a pawn used to measure response time?

Six months later, arrests were made in October. Breaking news hit of a foiled terrorist attack in Washington DC. Two arrests were made and many lives saved. The attack would have compromised structures, including a local popular restaurant. I was unaware of a plot to assassinate an embassy leader. There was also a plot to kill diners. This was the reason I kept picking up on the loss of many lives. The actual plans involved shooting or bombing those in the dining room within close proximity to the White House.

According to news stories, this terrorist attack lead was supplied to American officials in early May. I contacted police on May 2nd. I spent a couple of days speaking with officers over the phone. I don't know if my lead started things or if it confirmed other knowledge they already had. Authorities publicly claimed to have used intelligence agencies.

Points of interest were accurately flagged with appropriate capital letters. Areas involved were lit up and revealed. Letters and numbers were coordinates confirming targeted areas. The number "41" is a major route. A bomb was included in the attack on the restaurant. Occults referred to eastern descent. Diffused meant scattered local and abroad. The embassy building is close to the JFK building.

This whole situation brought back memories from the previous summer. I had had a reading booth at the local summer exposition. One evening, TJ and I strolled away from my booth for supper. We purchased a bucket of wings and found a picnic table to eat at. I sat enjoying the meal with TJ, until I became bombarded with visions of bloody violence.

This upheaval involved the people sitting at the table next to ours. The energy from these people was dark and terrifying. Most of them were well over six feet tall. They were loud, obnoxious and very crude. I overheard the ringleader utter "To death." Immediately I felt panicked. I needed to leave the table with TJ without them being aware.

I gently tapped TJ's toes under the table to get his attention. "I'm having a problem. The heat is bothering me. I need to get out of the sun now." I got up and started walking away. Instinctively TJ followed.

"What's wrong? You look like you've seen something horrific," TJ piped up, trying to figure out what was going on.

"I need to find a cop right now. Those people who sat beside us are gangsters. There's a gang fight going down immediately, inside the fairgrounds," we spotted an officer ahead. I picked up my pace and end up walking beside him.

"Excuse me, Officer."

"I'm busy with a situation. Find someone else." He was definitely on the same mission I was. He was desperately scanning the crowd as he walked. Only the party he was searching for was a quarter of a block behind him. I didn't need the bad guys see me talking to him either.

"Don't look at me." I kept pace with the officer and I looked straight ahead. "The seven black gang members are about a quarter of a block behind you near the corn shack. There's going to be a bloody gang fight with weapons and pepper spray. They'll be by a chain link fence. The leader is six foot five. He's wearing a bright pink T-shirt and black pants. There are five guys and two females back there at the green picnic tables."

"Thank you," the cop responded. He quickly turned into the cotton candy stand and then headed back in their direction.

TJ finally caught up to me. "I'm sorry I rushed ahead."

"He sure turned around in a hurry after you spoke to him. Did he say anything?

"He thanked me."

A bloody brawl between two gangs erupted shortly after, outside the chain link fence of the festival grounds. Several blaring sirens could be heard racing to the scene.

I heard through the grapevine that it took eight cop cars and five ambulances to clean up afterwards. The gangsters were either pepper sprayed or lacerated, if not both. One of the suspects was rendered unconscious.

I often receive unsolicited visions of upcoming situations. Exposure to terrorism is a newer level of intensity for me. Over five years ago, I warned a friend's father who was visiting Canada of a violent outburst that would happen in his community. He lived in the previously peaceful town of Maghar, Israel, beside the Sea of Galilee. Three weeks later the situation unfolded around him exactly as I had described. He and his wife fled to safety with only the clothes on their backs.

Spirit has shown me numerous murder cases. Important details are shown in black and white. I'm spared from having to see grotesque presentations. On occasion, I can actually hear the sounds and voices of what has or is about to go down. The killers are always shown to me in full color, as if they are standing directly in front of me.

Chapter Two

Silent Coordinates

Corrupt legal systems grossly interfere with delivering justice. Previously dedicated police officers have given up in frustration. This limits their participation in resolving crime. Policing has become substandard and dangerous. Convicts and murderers run among us committing horrendous crimes.

The story of a missing thirty year old parole officer hit the local news. Michael Black vanished into thin air, while running with a group of runners through the river valley. There was absolutely no trace of Michael, who stood over six feet tall and weighed 195 lbs. Search parties scoured the McLeod river valley in hopes of finding him.

I started putting things together; something was amiss. Michael wasn't the first person to go missing in the river valley lately. Unfortunately, he wasn't going to be the last. There had been a rash of recent deaths in this area. Authorities reported most of these cases as either suicide or accidental to prevent public panic.

In sheer frustration I called on my spirit guide. I closed my eyes, hoping to see what was really going on. When I close my eyes, a white screen appears. My 'third eye' is able to review any contents displayed on this screen.

"Is Michael Black alive?" I asked after a brief hesitation.

"N" was printed, meaning no.

"Did Michael commit suicide?" I asked.

"O." This meant no as well.

The phone rang, interrupting my trance.

The caller was Michael's sister Pattie. She wanted to know if I handled missing person's cases. I made arrangements to meet her at the entrance of the McLeod Park in an hour.

"TJ, I'm going out to help with the missing parole officer's case. Would you care to join me?" I asked my husband who was still watching the news.

"I'll tag along. I don't know how much good I'll be," TJ replied, turning off the TV.

While TJ drove, I sat quietly and shut my eyes hoping to connect with Michael. Within seconds the face of a sad weary ghost appeared to me. His skin was a grayish blue tone. Wisps of his ginger wavy hair lightly fell over his oblong forehead. His eyebrows drooped in despair as his eyelids blinked over his olive green eyes. He started to show me what had happened through a series of repeated visions.

Michael belonged to an elite racing group. Halfway into the early evening marathon, he stopped to tie his shoe. While squatting to tie his shoe, the call of nature struck him. The restrooms he urgently needed loomed in an accessible distance. He quickly approached the building and headed around the back of the building accessing the men's room. In a rush Michael firmly gripped the handle of the heavy metal door. The door was only opened a crack. A stranger from inside, whipped the door wide open. He stood glaring at Michael in a crazed, deranged, mocking manner.

This bald, stocky, shorter male of approximately forty years, continued to quietly taunt Michael for a couple more seconds. This weirdo's huge dark brown eyes were dilated as if he was high. His eyebrows darted up and down complimenting his devious attitude. Michael eventually darted past this disturbed man to use the facilities.

After answering the call of duty, he headed back outdoors hoping to catch up with the others. He sprinted through the semi-vacant parking lot. Then he jogged down the main path until it forked. A challenging muddy hill was to his right and his regular route was straight ahead. In seconds he throttled up the hill at great speed. Then he coasted down the other side of the hill which led back to the main path.

The moment Michael's pounding feet hit the deserted main pathway, he was ambushed by the psycho from the washroom. This deranged assailant grimaced and grunted, taking total control of his innocent victim. Being caught completely off guard, Michael was rendered defenseless. His attacker continued to shove him down the steep embankment. The parole officer panicked as he barreled out of control, just feet away from the river.

Michael relayed this to me in a military style. He displayed himself illuminated like the male figure shown on a pedestrian walk light, only he was three dimensional, solid white and running. The illusion resembled a humanoid image scrambling across a radar screen.

The sound of TJ's voice broke my connection with Michael.

"Laura, I'm not familiar with the river valley. Which route should I take?" TJ inquired patiently, waiting for my answer.

"Take the next exit up ahead. It leads to McLeod Park."

I closed my eyes hoping to reconnect with Michael. Just my luck he wasn't around. I knew from past experience that he would eventually return.

Minutes later we arrived at the park's main entrance and pulled into the main parking lot. Two women and a man quickly approached our vehicle. I took a couple of deep breaths before opening the car door.

"Hi, I'm Laura Laforce," I said reaching out to shake her hand. "You must be Pattie."

The young woman had been crying. Her beautiful blue eyes were bloodshot. Wisps of carrot red hair repeatedly spanked her face as the wind swirled around.

"I'm Pattie, Michael's sister." The gal was so distraught she could hardly speak. I opened my arms offering a comforting hug. After a brief hug, the other lady stepped forward.

I'm Trista," piped up the other woman.

"Douglas," uttered the man who stood next to her. "Folks, meet my husband TJ, a medium as well."

"Is Michael alive?" Pattie inquired with a dash of hope on her face.

I hesitated briefly before answering her.

"Pattie, I'm sorry he's dead."

"Are you sure?" she asked before starting to sob.

"Yes, one hundred percent positive," I replied, allowing her time to digest the truth. "He's already come to me. Only souls who've passed approach me in the manner Michael did."

"Could you be wrong?" she implored.
"No," I stated, looking directly in her eyes.

Despair and tension filled the evening air. I stepped back, allowing Pattie and her friends a few minutes to compose themselves. Emotionally this was going to be a tough one. I instantly knew what my purpose was going to be and it wasn't going to be great. My job was to piece together the crime. Finding Michael's body wasn't going to be easy.

"Laura, I have Michael's jacket. Would it help to hold it?" Pattie hollered over the wind.

"Probably not," I answered.

Pattie desperately hurled his jacket like a javelin towards me. I caught the jacket in midair and bundled it in my arms. This fleecy garment began bursting with energy. I could see golden sparks. It felt as if pop rocks went off in my hands. Michael was instantly back.

"Do you know what happened to my brother?" Pattie inquired.

"I need time to piece together what Michael was trying to show me," I replied in all honesty. "There was something about a bald man and a heavy metal washroom door."

"Was there anything else?" she begged.

"Yes, he was running and there was a fork in the path. He took the hill at record breaking speed. After reaching the summit, he veered down the hill. Once he reached the main path, he was jumped and forced down the river bank. He plummeted out of control towards the rushing river. I don't have any more right now," I answered, trying to share all I'd been shown.

"Can you contact him again?" she asked.

"I will let you know when there's more to share," I informed her.

Reporters arrived on the scene. Thankfully, we were able to avoid them. A few hungry people wanted the spotlight. I didn't need to draw unwanted attention to myself with a murderer being loose in the park.

"We're going to stay awhile and help with the search," I told the party of three. "I want everyone to stay together or within eyesight of each other. If anyone sees a bald man with brown eyes and dark brown eyelashes let me know right away."

"Excuse me, Laura, about an hour ago a bald man on a bicycle stopped to talk to me. He asked if I was with the search party. After I confirmed my involvement, the guy told me there were four old coal mines in the area," Douglas mentioned.

I shut my eyes to link up with Spirit. "Was that the killer that this searcher encountered?" Everything lit up, meaning yes.

"This person who approached you is the killer. He gets off mingling among the searchers. Please avoid him, but don't let on that you know what he's done."

Before leaving the parking lot, I excused myself with TJ to check out the washroom door, making sure it matched up to what I was shown. I needed to validate what I was shown before carrying on.

We reunited with the group and started walking across another adjoining parking lot. This was weird. Last week I was shown two dark public parking lots. The signs were black, indicating death. I kept the vision in the back of my mind realizing it would eventually be important.

TV reporters were doing an interview with another family member on a nearby deck, which stood over the river. I stepped up and took a seat on a nearby bench. The soles of my feet burned like they were on fire. I kept feeling a firm downward tug. Michael's ghost printed a huge black letter "W" in midair followed the number 3. He was trying to tell me something, but I didn't understand.

I quickly returned to the group and quietly asked TJ to check out the deck. TJ quietly sauntered off to the deck and sat where I had been. Minutes later he returned to us.

"TJ, did you get anything?" I asked.

"Yes, I had a strong pull from under my feet," TJ responded.

Before carrying on, another group of eight friends of Michael rushed over to join us. Pattie introduced TJ and me to the group, mentioning we were mediums. Thirteen people gathered around preparing to assist in the search for Michael. Shortly after heading down the trail, the questions started to fly.

"Is Michael alive?" asked one of the girls.

"Did Michael commit suicide?" questioned his cousin.

"Is it true that he went crazy and ran off somewhere?" an older lady asked.

"Did he fall prey to an organ harvester?"

These people were desperate and extremely upset. They deserved to know what had happened. I needed to be careful with how I handled this delicate situation. I didn't want to jeopardize the group's safety or risk the word getting out too soon about the murder. I wasn't sure if the killing was random or pre-meditated.

"Can I have everyone please gather into a tight circle," I directed.

I quickly scanned every individual in the group making sure they were all uninvolved in the crime. I also didn't want anyone leaking information to anyone who might be indirectly or directly connected to the case.

"I'm sorry. The news isn't good." I briefly paused. "Michael is dead. He's been murdered."

"Oh, My God, no," cried out one of the ladies before she broke down sobbing. Several members of the group gathered around comforting her.

"He can't be dead. He's a big strapping guy. You can't be right," one of the guys snapped.

"Everybody loves Michael," another girl piped up. "He doesn't have any enemies."

"How do you know he's dead?" a guy from the group responded, as he stood, fighting back the tears in his eyes.

"Michael appeared to me. He showed me important details about the circumstances before I arrived at the park."

"How do you know it's him for sure?" he questioned.

"Don't all these so called spirits look the same?"

"His appearance matched his missing picture on the flyers," I responded.

I spent some time with the group comforting and consoling them. They needed to compose themselves before we could continue the search.

"Who killed him?" Trista asked.

"There's a bald man in the park. He's between the age of thirty five and forty five. The murderer is shorter than Michael and husky. He has dark brown eyes and eye brows. This predator makes direct eye contact with his victims while taunting them with grunting noises."

"Do you know where Michael is?" Douglas asked.

"No, I was disrupted while communicating with him. But I have reason to believe he's in the river."

"Hey, I found Michael's favorite drink can beside the path," Douglas announced.

"This is freaking me out. Is he trying to mark the way with hints?"

"Douglas, consider these clues as your friend's way of communicating," I mentioned, hoping he'd calm down. "Your friend Michael wants to be found."

"Laura, look over there on the ground by the bushes," Trista pointed in excitement. "Michael went missing on the 8th of June. Could this be another clue?"

A city bus transfer was lying face up undisturbed with a huge number eight on it.

"Yes, he's giving us clues."

"Is he with us now?" she asked.

"Yes."

I never told Michael's family or friends that he was a ghost. They didn't need more heart wrenching news to deal with. Thank God no one asked if he was okay or happy. This would have made the situation more difficult for them.

"What the hell?" Pattie shouted in anger and despair. "Why are people tearing down the missing persons posters that I've hung up? Don't they care?"

"I know this is hard to cope with. It's nothing personal. Young punks out having fun don't think of others. They don't realize how disrespectful their actions are," I calmly mentioned, hoping to ease her tension.

"Come check this out!" Douglas hollered, waving his hands in the air. "Someone wrote Michael's initials in the dirt on the path."

The group rushed over to Douglas, gathering around to view the unusual display of initials "MB" etched into the path. These initials were at least a foot long and a foot wide.

"Could Michael do this?" Douglas asked.

"Yes, Michael did this," I replied.

"Look, there's something drawn underneath his initials, that "K" resembles a map." Douglas exclaimed in excitement.

"Laura, have you seen these types of drawings before?" Pattie asked, staring me directly in the eye.

"Many times it's easier for deceased loved ones to communicate with us this way," I explained.

"Drawings like these are important."

We looked over the drawing, attempting to decipher this map as a group. My take of the details was the blank area contained his body. All the lines were solid, except for a blank circle drawn in the middle of the "K". This drawing also somewhat resembled the dirt packed path surrounding us. The group took turns sharing their interpretation of the map.

In the distance, sticks could be heard breaking above us in the brush up the hill. A scruffy dirty blonde male with a beard was watching the group from a distance. He quickly retreated into the bush and was replaced by a husky native male with a huge moustache. He stood silently observing the group. Number three had been shown earlier on. I wondered if these two men were somehow tied to the crime. Perhaps they knew of the predator and his slayings.

Pattie reached out and quietly tapped me on the shoulder.

"Do you want me to check out those guys up there?" she offered in a heartbeat.

"Please stay here with us," I demanded. "The energy coming from them is negative."

We continued the search until sunset. TJ and I headed home tired and exasperated.

"Remember last year, Spirit showed me a guy in camouflage gear running to and fro in a bush area. After that a violent man held him to the ground with some sort of stick handle. Two other men were near the scene," TJ reminded me.

"Come to think of it, I recall you mentioning this a long time ago."

We sat in silence the rest of the way home, while I tried to, piece together all the clues. In my opinion finding the killer was going to be far easier than finding Michael's body.

"Shall I put on the tea-kettle for us?" TJ asked, heading toward the kitchen.

"Sounds like a plan. I'm going to draw a bath while the water boils. After we have tea, I'll go soak in the tub and try to reconnect with Michael."

"Isn't it odd how water seems to heighten your connections with the other side?" TJ curiously stated.

"I don't understand why, but being in the water brings better clarity. The relaxation changes my vibrations. Perhaps it's the combination of flesh, water and air with no barriers."

"It's definitely different," TJ said.

Shortly after pouring the bubble bath, I disrobed and slid into the mirage of bubbles. The aroma of sweet hibiscus steamed through the air. I rested my head against the back of the tub and shut my eyes. Minutes later, Michael appeared.

"Michael, what happened?" I asked.

Michael started to show me black and white scenes of the activities surrounding his death. A shovel with a knee high handle was revealed. His body was shoved at a slant and pushed with great ease into a dark void. Behind the action was a wall like a river bank. This almost seemed easy like pushing a boat away from a pier, but only into something instead. He repeated this twice before vanishing.

The river had already been dragged by professionals with nets. Could several teams somehow miss finding a body in the water? Probably not! I thought to myself. Could he be packed into a suitcase and sunk to the bottom? This would be unrealistic due to his large size. If there was a slanted hole or culvert he may have been easily pushed into that, but he should have appeared slumped over instead. I decided no big mysteries were going to be solved tonight. Pulling the plug I left the tub to drain. I headed into our cozy dim lit bedroom where TJ lay waiting for me.

"Was anything spectacular revealed during your bath?" TJ inquired.

"Yes, a handsome sexy man known to me was waiting between my bed sheets."

"Oh, you're so bad!" TJ teased.

We cuddled for a few moments before falling asleep.

I was in the middle of a pleasant dream when I was awakened by my spirit guide. A vision of Michael's face was revealed. His face was distorted, pale and mostly covered with white rocks. I went back to sleep; there was nothing I could do. In the morning I headed back to the park to meet up with Pattie.

"Hi Laura, do you have anything new?" Pattie asked.

"Yes, but there is still a lot of searching to do. I don't always understand everything I'm being shown. Things seem to be revealed in pieces."

"Do you think we'll find him?" Pattie questioned.

"He will be found, but not right away. Sometimes it takes weeks to work through something like this."

"Can't you ask his guides for help?" she inquired.

"Yes, but I need to be able to understand what I'm being shown. It's not as easy as they make it look on TV."

"Laura, this park's been searched and the river dragged. Yesterday another psychic told me that he's in the trunk of a car a hundred miles north of town. What do you think about that? Do you think someone drove his body out of the park?" Pattie sat studying my face, probably hoping that I would agree with the woman.

"I don't agree with what was said. If a vehicle was involved, I would have seen it right away. I don't let the opinion of others affect my work. There are many charlatans out there who claim to be psychics." Pattie was desperate and grasping for straws, hoping for a better outcome.

"This elderly gypsy lady has been doing readings for years. I went to see her out of desperation for a tarot reading hoping to find my brother. I shuffled the cards and she laid them out in a spread. Right away the death card came up followed by a four of swords with a coffin on it, which was followed by a card with a chariot on it." Pattie went on about this person's presentation.

"Is that all she based her answer on?" I asked her, while pushing back my feelings on what this reader was doing.

"Yes," Pattie replied.

I felt disappointed that a psychic had taken advantage of Pattie in her delicate state. She probably even charged her a fair chunk of change. In the meanwhile I'm out in the bush, volunteering my services and helping her.

"Pattie, you can't get answers from a tarot deck unless the reader is gifted. It isn't realistic. Those are only cards with pictures drawn on them and nothing more. If you want an accurate reading I'll give you one. I will hold your hands and close my eyes. Then I will share with you what is disclosed."

"I'll get back to you on that. Laura, excuse me for changing the subject, but there are two groups of us searching today," Pattie started, before pulling out her map. "The other searchers have headed towards the Westgate Park Point. What action do you think we should take?"

"I think we should be searching east of the parking lot from the riverbank to the hilltop for the next kilometer. We should be looking for anything that has been disturbed," I mentioned before we headed out on the path.

I started feeling weak and sick. I needed to take a break. Pattie sat quietly nearby patiently waiting for me. While sitting on a log I closed my eyes. I received a vision of a black rectangle with white letter "S," marking something significant in the middle.

I opened my eyes for a few minutes trying to digest what I was shown. With my eyes open, I spotted a vision of a white beam in the hill above us. Then a flare-like image lit up the sky to the right of this hilltop. This was followed by an orange beam hovering over the river. These three light images revealed important locations.

I shut my eyes hoping to receive more information. Two black coded messages of "23K" and "35 SS" were displayed repeatedly. These seemed to be coordinates.

"Pattie, does "23K" or "35 SS" mean anything to you?" I asked straightening my back.

"Michael used to be in the army years ago and those could be either codes or coordinates," she informed me.

"Keep those in mind. They may come in useful later."

"Are you almost done resting?" Pattie asked, becoming quite restless.

"Yes, let's head further up the trail." I agreed as I gradually peeled myself off the rugged log that I'd been sitting on.

We got back on our feet and headed down the straight path, which was starting to curve. Shortly after entering the bend we discovered a fallen log. A large etching the size of a fist read "23K," which pointed like an arrow towards the river. We stopped to examine the etching on the trunk and took everything into consideration.

"Spirit, please help us with this. I don't understand," I quietly begged.

"This means something, doesn't it, Laura?" Pattie questioned, pushing for answers.

"Yes, but I don't quite understand. I try not to jump to conclusions when things like this are happening."

"What do we do now?" she quizzed, adjusting her cap.

"We keep going. There's obviously more to this. Michael needs to be found and his killer arrested."

The noise of running footsteps could be heard rushing towards us on the path.

"Hey girls, wait up," Douglas shouted with a raspy breathless voice. "Have you had any luck over here?"

"We need to explore the hilltop over there. Would you help us?" I asked, hoping he could help us with the next area. "I'm not in good physical condition. I don't even know if I can make it up there."

"What's wrong?" Douglas asked.

"Something keeps pinching me deep inside and putting everything into spasm," I told them.

"Should you be out here doing this?" Pattie's tone changed to that of genuine concern.

"Nobody should. There's a murderer at large here in the river valley." I had no intention of backing out of the search.

"Are you okay enough to go further?" she probed. "Yes, we need to do this," I answered.

The three of us started heading up the steep hill. I started to stumble through the rough terrain. I ended up losing my footing for a few seconds. I landed on a soft hilly ground covered by leaves, which gently delivered me to a safer plateau. It was almost like sliding through feathers.

"Are you okay?" Pattie shouted.

"I'm fine."

"You looked as if you were riding a toboggan," she giggled, tripping over the next stump herself and falling flat on her ass.

"That's what I call divine intervention returning the favor," I snickered as she pulled herself to her feet.

I was hoping everything would be okay. I started to head back up the hill to catch up with them. Three weeks earlier, I had spent the night in emergency, but weakness wasn't an excuse I was willing to own. I grabbed onto the trunk of tree not knowing that it was hollow. The darn thing fell over right in front of my legs, scraping up my shins.

Pattie and I decided to take a break for a few minutes halfway up the hill and sat on the plateau, while Douglas continued on ahead of us.

"Can you help me talk to my brother?" Pattie asked.

"Lay back and close your eyes. Ask Michael to come to you," I guided her while I lay beside her on the ground.

"Ask him to give you a symbol you can recognize him by."

"He's lightly brushing the top of my head," Pattie announced. "I can smell his stinky socks."

"Could someone come here?" Douglas shouted, interrupting our session.

"Did you find Michael?" Pattie shouted.

"No, but this should be checked out," Douglas eagerly replied, tearing through whatever he had found.

Pattie rushed over to Douglas. I gradually plodded up the hill. The moment I reached the top, I discovered the dark rectangle with an "S" in the middle that I had seen in an earlier vision. The rectangle previously revealed was a rectangular shaped makeshift lair with a dirt base and dirt walls. It turns out, the "S," was a knee-high handled shovel, standing between a pair of expensive clean work boots. The three of us were walking through the homeless man's home.

We had reached the killer's den. My heart surged with adrenaline as we searched the makeshift home for clues. His lair was meticulous, practical, and army-like. At the edge of this shelter was a woven fire pit, which resembled an oblong beaver dam.

Douglas started picking through the fire pit. He discovered a pair of scissors gently resting among the logs and picked them up. A ginger strand of hair remained clasped between the two blades. Douglas suddenly sneezed, releasing the evidence into the pit below. Pattie and I shifted a couple of logs hoping to retrieve the piece of fallen hair. It was apparent that he used this fire pit to hold his personal effects. There was a toothbrush, razor, shaving cream, and soap, but no brush or comb.

Douglas started searching through the tidy bags of belongings, which lined the adjacent dirt wall. Then he carelessly shoved the clothing back into plastic shopping bags. This beast was going to know his belongings had been disturbed.

"I feel like I'm going to puke," Pattie mentioned while holding her stomach.

"This place makes me feel ill," Douglas stated.

The dark energy in this area was nauseating them. Everything was matching up to what I had been shown.

"We had better get out of here before he comes back," I demanded feeling uneasy. "I'm having trouble with my stomach again. It keeps going into spasm. I don't think I could outrun this killer in my condition. " I started toward the edge of the steep hill.

"Let's go," Pattie shouted.

The three of us trekked down the hill, just shy of neck-breaking speed. My legs were unstable and wobbly. I could only imagine how the others felt.

"Is everybody ready to head back to the parking lot? I need to find a bathroom."

"Why don't you use the bush? We're a long way from the restrooms," Pattie mentioned.

"I would, but nothing's private enough."

"There a clump of brush and nobody will see." Douglas pointed a short distance away. "We'll stay over here."

I reluctantly excused myself, taking the opportunity but dreading every single moment. I felt extremely vulnerable with a killer at large in the park. On the way back through the brush the others obviously heard me making my way back towards them.

"Hey Laura, is that you?" Douglas's loud voice boomed as I almost reached the clearing.

I briefly considered making some sort of smart remark, but chose not to. "Yes, I'm still alive."

Pattie made her way over to me. "Do you think Michael will be found soon? If he's dead I need to see his body in order to believe it."

"Yes, he'll be found, but I don't know if you'll be allowed to view him."

An hour later, we finally arrived back at the main parking lot. Constant pain kept pulsating under my ribcage. Visible cuts and scratches decorated my legs. Blisters burned the bottoms of my feet. There was another group of searchers coming from the opposite direction as we headed towards our vehicles.

"Hey, guys. Wait up," a muffled voice hollered from a distance.

"Did you find anything?" Douglas shouted.

The rest of the group from yesterday sauntered over to meet us. Before retiring for the day, both groups exchanged their latest findings. A couple of new faces had joined in the search. A petite girl walked up to Pattie and reached out her arms offering her a hug.

"I'm sorry about Michael," the girl spoke. "I've heard he's been murdered. Is there a description of the killer?"

Pattie was overcome with emotion. She stepped away, trying to contain herself.

"We're looking for a bald man with brown eyes in his mid thirties to forties," Douglas replied.

"Holy shit," she freaked looking as if she'd seen a ghost.

"What's wrong?" Douglas probed.

"Earlier today our group was gathered over there by the benches. A bald man matching that description was hiding behind those trees watching us. I thought he was a reporter or perhaps a curious bystander," she confessed.

"Are you crazy or something? Reporters are thirsty for news. I can't believe you think they'd hide behind trees." Pattie spoke loudly with tears welling in her eyes. "What sort of idiot are you?"

"That rotten dirty bastard is taking pride in this. He's getting a rise out of the misery he's causing us." Douglas started kicking at the gravel in the parking lot.

"How could he do this to my brother? How could anybody do this? He's evil. If I catch him first he's dead. I'll kill him with my bare hands." Pattie yelled in anguish.

"I'll show him." She started heading towards the path that led to the killer's den.

"He's going to die. I'll kill that rotten bastard myself."

"Pattie stop, please come back, he's not worth killing." Doug's hoarse voice shouted behind her.

"Let's report this to the cops instead."

"Pattie, Doug's right. You need to call the detective who's working your brother's case. I want you to tell him about everything," I told her.

"Tonight I'm going to place a call to Crime Hotline with similar details. Hopefully the cops are going to take us seriously."

I received an eerie call that evening. A man on the phone was requesting a reading for that night. He went on to tell me this would be the only time he'd ever be able to see me. His sister was in town and he could get a ride. Immediately I sensed an evil darkness. I shut my eyes and Spirit revealed the murderer's face. In an instant I had confirmed the caller was the killer. I told him I wasn't taking appointments and abruptly hung up disconnecting him. Panic started to take over. I worried about my safety. I asked my guide and the angels to protect me and the other innocent people.

Receiving this upsetting call kicked me into action. I found the number for the snitch line and started dialing it. The lady answering the phone didn't seem overly interested in what I had to say.

"The missing persons division is closed over the weekend. They probably won't see this until Tuesday or Wednesday," the lady absently rattled off.

"I'm calling in about a homicide. Why are you downgrading this urgent situation?"

"Missing people can't be upgraded to homicide without a body," she insisted.

"That's not true. What about the Rogers? They were assumed murdered. Eventually a judge legally declared them dead, even though their bodies have never been found."

"I'm sorry, I have to pass this on to missing persons, because they're handling this file."

"I feel like you're passing the buck. Can't you bend the rules this time? In my eyes, this sort of policing is unacceptable and irresponsible."

"Sorry."

"How many more need to die at the hands of this serial killer?" I challenged her.

"I have to let you go," she said. "I have another call coming in."

"Can I please have your name?" I asked.

"I'm sorry, we don't supply our names," she stated in a harsh tone.

"Sorry I asked, other officers have provided a first name in the past. Can I have the file number?"

I could hear her sigh in dread before she supplied the numbers I requested. After revealing them she released me from her line. Her cold conduct left me feeling frustrated.

I picked up the phone and called Pattie to see how far she had gotten with the detective.

"Did you get anywhere with the police?" I asked while grabbing a paper pad to jot things down on.

"No, the detective assigned to this case was being a real ass," she started to sob. "He told me I was under the microscope as a possible suspect."

"Don't worry about what that jerk said. He's harmlessly useless. Everybody knows you're innocent. I despise cops who purposely torment victims. Did you tell him about the bald homeless ex-military man who lives close to the hilltop in a den? Did you mention the clean short handled shovel and the clean work boots leaning against the wall?"

"Yes, he told me that man has been living there for quite some time. Eventually this detective became irritated with me and said that he'd go interview him tomorrow."

My intuition told me this cop had no interest in carrying out any sort of interview with the homeless villain.

"I keep feeling Michael around me tonight. It's almost like he's touching my shoulder. Why is this happening?"

"He's trying to comfort you," I reassured her.

We talked awhile. After hanging up, I headed to the living room to spend time with my husband.

TJ and I sat together snuggling in front of the television unwinding from our busy day. Excruciating waves of pain suddenly seized my body. My stomach became rock hard and bloated to twice its size. TJ rushed to the medicine cabinet and returned with my painkillers.

"These should help," TJ said while he handed me a couple of tablets and a glass of water.

Forty-five minutes passed and my condition started to worsen. Breathing became extremely difficult. Something was attacking my insides.

"I don't understand why those pills aren't working. If this doesn't stop in a few minutes I'll have to rush you to the hospital."

TJ sat quietly with me trying to ease the pain with his healing abilities. Suddenly he started exhibiting signs of physical distress.

"Oh my God, my head hurts," freaked TJ, struggling to contain himself. "It just came to me that this killer is psychically inclined. When I figured out you were under the spell of a dark psychic attack, I tried to release you. In frustration the killer turned his focus on my head. The pressure is so intense it feels like my head is going to explode."

"Surround us and protect us, Spirit. Send in the angels to help us," we both requested.

"Laura, that murderer is using black magic on us.

"He's trying to harm you, because you're onto him. He turned on me in anger when I caught on to what he was doing to you. We need to be more cautious. You are a threat to this very dangerous man."

"Earlier today, I saw a vision of a black stomach, but I paid no attention to it," I mentioned.

"Why would you ignore something like that?" TJ asked with a look of shock on his face.

"I was trying to resolve a murder and find a body. A black stomach didn't belong."

"Did you brush off anything else?" TJ questioned, grasping the edge of the couch to pull himself into a better position.

"Yes, I was shown a pink drawing, which resembled a colon like image on a medical anatomy chart. There was a black X at the top and a black X placed at the bottom of the organ.

"You ignored that vision knowing those aren't good colours?" TJ grimaced, glancing at my stomach.

"I thought it had to do with my health at first, until we came across a curved staircase with ridges, which closely resembled the drawing. Those particular stairs lead us towards the killer's lair. That was when I decided to add it to the rest of the clues in the case."

I awoke early in the morning after a sound sleep. Before I opened my eyes, I was shown a vision of Michael's lifeless body lying on the riverbank. White fist sized rocks lay close to his head. Beside him were two forensic workers dressed in white. Michael was lying face up with his arms positioned across his chest. He was dressed mostly in black, but something white was attached to the front of him. His ginger wavy hair was now muddy and straight. My view would have been from approximately 30 feet away. The skin tone from a distance was unusual. There were no mounds of dirt around him, yet the dark void still existed close by. A riverbank wall could be seen in the background behind him.

"TJ, Michael's body is going to be found shortly," I announced, waking up my husband from a sound sleep.

"Will you find him?"

"Probably not, but I'm okay with that. I don't know if I could handle seeing that first hand."

"What if you did find him?" TJ questioned. "Obviously, I'd have to cope with it," I replied.

I remained in bed contemplating what I'd seen. The newest vision definitely led me to the riverbank. I couldn't understand why we were coming up empty handed. I started reviewing the other clues, but I didn't know where these fit in.

Michael communicated in army-like codes using coordinates. This was unusual and confusing for me, because there were numbered markers along the river valley which could easily correspond. All I knew for sure was Michael had been murdered. I saw the killer and where he lived. Everything else was revealed in bits and pieces.

I needed to get cracking this morning. Pattie and I were meeting back at the park at ten. The moment we met, the questions started to fly.

"Laura, do you think Michael's going to be found?" Pattie asked, tying her hair back into a ponytail.

"Yes, I was shown them recovering his body."

"Is he found alive?"

"No Pattie, he's dead. A forensic team wearing white suits are on site beside his lifeless body," I answered, hoping she'd understand.

"Maybe he's hurt and they're helping him. Have you ever seen anything like that before?"

"Yes, several times. This always means the body will be found within days."

"I hope you're wrong. You're the only psychic who says he's dead," she growled with a snarky undertone. "I talked with another psychic here in town last night. She told me he was alive and living in the bush. Then I called one in the States. This lady also told me he was alive and had taken up with another girl. After that, I spoke with a Reikki master from the States. She said he was alive, but had lost his memory after hurting his head. This woman performed long distance healing on him with an empty Reikki bed. I spent a lot of money last night trying to find him."

"Remember another one told you he was in the trunk of a car north of town. Another intuitive told you he was in a basement of a house on the south side and even provided you with a physical address," I said, briefly summarizing the details.

"You've always said that he was dead. You keep saying he was murdered in the park, but you've never told me exactly how." She added, "One of those other psychics told me he didn't want me to know where he was. Did he tell you to keep it from me?"

"I've been shown bits and pieces of what happened. I'm human and I don't see everything." I felt myself becoming exasperated being badgered this way. It took everything I had not to engage in any sort of argument with her. "Michael will be found shortly. I'm here for you if you need me."

"What really doesn't make sense is that we haven't found him."

"Yes, this situation is hard. Things can take a long time to piece together. You've probably noticed that I've been working with other intuitives. These people are trustworthy, but that doesn't always give us what we need right away. Many clues are matching up, but deciphering them can be tricky."

"I'm sorry about snapping," she apologized.

"It's kind of odd that you keep saying he's dead and your story never changes. You've spent days and countless hours helping me search for Michael. You've never asked me for a cent. You even refused to accept cash from my aunt."

"It's unethical for me to charge you for services in your dire circumstances. I'm here to help. These feelings that you're having are normal. Anger is part of the grieving process," I told her.

"Have you ever said someone was dead and they turned up alive?"

"Never."

"You haven't wavered or changed your answers. Could you be wrong?" she quizzed.

"No, Michael has appeared to me several times. Only the dead manifest like that. We'd better get heading back. I'm surprised they haven't found him yet. They'll be finding him shortly."

I heard on the news, a month later, that Michael had been found. His remains were found washed up on the river bank; twenty three kilometers upstream from where we'd been searching. Authorities identified Michael's badly decomposed remains through his dental records.

I called Pattie to offer her my condolences.

"Hi, Pattie. I heard the news. Is there anything I can do for you?" I offered.

"It's been so hard lately. I feel like I want to die," she said.

"It's like dealing with his loss all over again. They're refusing to tell us how he died, except that he drowned."

I knew she wasn't suicidal. I could feel her pain. She was mourning, releasing her hurt and anger.

"Loss is never easy, especially when you're close to the person."

"Is my brother okay?" she asked.

"He's at rest," I assured her.

"Can I still talk to him like we did at the park?"

"You can talk to him like you always did. Call me if you need anything. I'm here for you," I told her.

"Thank you," she said, before hanging up the phone.

Michael appeared to me later in the evening, as I started to fall asleep. He finally showed me exactly how he was killed. Two black stick figures were used to re-enact the previously undisclosed pieces of his murder. After being jumped, Michael was stumbling uncontrollably down the steep embankment towards the river. His assailant forcefully hit Michael diagonally between the shoulder blades with the short handle of the shovel. The back of his head and neck may have been clipped during the attack. When Michael scurried to his feet the man pushed him face first to the ground. This identical assault was repeated once more. The predator dragged the unconscious parole officer's body to the edge of the water and effortlessly submerged him.

After witnessing this I became restless. I leapt out of bed and headed to my office across the hall. I needed to finish piecing together all the visions and coded messages from this case. Understanding this could help me to better assist others in the future.

I grabbed the local map and opened it to view the river valley. The drawing in the dirt and the map in my hand perfectly coincided with the narrow line representing the river He was found twenty three kilometers away from the park, which was etched on the fallen log we came across weeks ago. This broken stump had pointed toward the water. The letter "T" told how he was hit (T-boned) and "P" means pushed. Number "7" accurately indicated his point of entry into the water. I spotted a green marker with the number "7" painted on it directly across the river. He was found south of secondary highway "35 S" near a cove, which resembled the blank area on the map. "W" stood for water and the black void was the river. The rocks covering his face meant he wasn't buried. His body washed up on the bank of the river valley with rocks near his head. His hair was straight because it was wet and his skin waterlogged.

The number "3" refers to three people being aware. The killer is one of them. The other two men are homeless. They are not involved, but they know what he did.

Attending the site helped to locate the weapon. We were also able to pinpoint the whereabouts of his killer, but were unable to do more.

The police initially refused to release his cause of death. Afterwards they tried passing off his demise as suicide. Later they claimed it was an accidental drowning. The police misled the public by telling reporters that no useful leads had come in.

Presently we have a serial killer at large. Several dead bodies have turned up in this river valley at different locations. He preys upon males and females. One of these recent murders was committed by a sharp edged tool. This shovel is the weapon in question. It even fits the damage done to the other victim. Our police have been informed, but they refuse to look any further.

Chapter Three
Triage

Predators constantly prey on the innocent, creating more victims as the hours roll by. They survive like mobsters on the inside. The offenders keep resurfacing on the outside. The prisons have revolving doors. Punishments are minuscule, if carried out. Prison guards fear for their lives.

Policing has become both corrupt and ineffective. Police chiefs, sergeants and detectives have succumbed to inner bullying. They obey the hierarchy within, hoping to avoid conflict.

The Crime Hotlines are operated by constables around the continent. I've discovered through experience that many Canadian calls are routed to the United States to be answered. These leads are sent to various triage teams who decide what fits their protocol.

Sweltering afternoon sun reddened our bare arms as TJ navigated the busy freeway. Our Nissan passed under the same pedestrian overpass from which teenagers dropped a boulder, killing a taxi driver several years earlier. The situation could have been dealt with sooner had I reported the vision I saw. I even knew what they looked like and where they hung out. It ended up taking the police a few years to arrest the three youths involved.

Shortly after passing by the old crime scene, a fresh unrelated vision appeared. A life-sized male with black hair and brown eyes was wearing a red bandana. The red scarf indicated a very dangerous man.

"Guess what, TJ?" I perked up.

"You love me?" he answered in a joking manner, swerving to avoid the blown tire lying ahead in our lane.

"Yes I love you, but this scary strange life-sized man was just shown to me."

"Is he a future soul mate?" TJ questioned in a ridiculous tone.

"No, he's a murderer." A thick rash of validating chills covered my flesh.

"How can you be so sure?" TJ quizzed while trying to keep up with both me and the traffic.

"I'm always shown dangerous people in full color, especially murderers. I don't understand why I need to see him. I can't see who he's killed and I probably can't help anyways," I explained while scrutinizing the freeway in case this suspect might be nearby.

"I was shown to you in full colour and I'm not dangerous," TJ replied, rapidly braking to make room between us and the vehicle that cut in. "Young drivers these days just don't think. I almost clipped him."

"Good thing you're cautious on the road, but back to the vision. It was different when Spirit showed you to me." I started relaxing my tense shoulders against my slightly reclined front seat.

"I don't understand," TJ whimpered in a ridiculous whiny boy's voice.

TJ's boyish affects didn't complement something so serious. I knew he was trying to lighten the mood.

Choosing to ignore his childish antics, I grabbed my notepad and ballpoint pen out of the glove box. I started jotting down all the physical traits and impressions of this dangerous man. I'd been shown this person for a reason. Eventually the information would come in handy.

"Does the cat have your tongue?" my driver whispered, desperately trying to penetrate the silence.

"Never," I said, after a moment of silence. I went back to finishing my notes while the vision was still fresh.

Several days later, while out on my daily walk, my eyes spotted a missing persons bulletin displayed on the front page of the newspaper. Out of curiosity I bought a copy. I took a few moments to study the photo of the elderly couple. I started reading the story pasted directly below their picture.

Local Elderly Couple Missing

Nancy and Allan Rogers went missing somewhere between Alberta and BC on Monday, August 10th. The couple was last seen fuelling their RV at the Costless Gas and Splash in Edmonton. They failed to arrive at their destination 3 days ago. If you happen to see them please have them call home.

My heart went out to this family. I could feel the agony this poor family faced, desperately searching for their parents.

My sixth sense started kicking into gear. I started slipping into an inevitable trance. My energy started to fluctuate. Feeling a little lightheaded, I wanted a place to relax.

A huge oak tree stood in the middle of the park facing a pond. Under this tree sat a vacant wooden bench. This setting seemed the perfect invitation. Increasing my pace, I arrived at the tree in seconds. I sought refuge under the huge oak boughs plunking myself onto the weathered seat, while the leaves above gently rustled in the breeze.

A translucent woman's body started to manifest on the seat beside me. She resembled the missing woman.

"Are you Nancy Rogers?" I already knew, but I wanted validation from her. She nodded her head in agreement. Visions of her dire situation projected like a slide show.

An elongated small letter "f" was displayed lying on its side, with the opening of the curve facing down.

The line which crossed the alphabetical letter appeared much higher up than usual. A raised circular extension jutted out from the top of the hook. This was not an actual letter, but a map of her whereabouts.

In the following frame the man's face I had seen days before on the freeway surfaced again. A stretch of highway was revealed with a village on each end. A dead end sign stood erect by a barbed wire fence north of the entrance. A wilderness bog hid a major highway from the scene.

Next she revealed different angles of a murky body of water, not the innocent pond which sat before me. The slough contained several small islands covered in tall yellow grass. Trenches filled with filthy water surrounded these pieces of land, like moats to a sand castle.

"Nancy how did this happen?" I sat concentrating on her with my eyes remaining shut.

Movie-like scenes played the events to my third eye:

Her husband Allan gently braked their RV and pulled into a country store. The slowing motion aroused Nancy, disturbing her afternoon nap. Out of mild curiosity she briefly opened her eyes scrutinizing the dingy stop. The stucco premises was run down and ragged. A classic beverage sign creaked in the wind, slightly above the entrance. With a lack of interest she adjusted her travel pillow and reclined back into her cushy front seat falling sound asleep.

Mr. Rogers exited the vehicle, gently closing the driver side door. Allan entered the store as a scruffy man exited. While the senior grazed the confectionary searching for treats, the dangerous stranger previously shown to me entered their motorhome through the unlocked side door. Keeping low, he squatted down hiding in its stairwell. He synchronized his breathing to match that of the sleeping woman reclining slightly above him.

Mrs. Rogers had become accustomed to her husband's frequent stops and habits. The villain calmly positioned himself beneath his first victim's seat. He gently located her seatbelt between the dark open crevice of passenger's seat and her side door. Tilting his head he could see the direction the restraint rested on her body through the rearview mirror. He noticed a drawstring with a loop dangling to the left side.

A few minutes later, Allan climbed back into his driver's seat. He drove away turning up his favorite tunes. Both hands were on the wheel in the nine o'clock and three o'clock positions. The right hand was glued in position. His left hand vigorously tapped to the beat as Nancy lightly snored.

The predator slid his left index finger through the loop. He used his right hand to skillfully raise the safety belt to her throat. He secured the crisscrossed seatbelt and drawstring into position. Then he started to manipulate both strangling devices from the passenger's backside like a puppeteer. Firmly grasping each side like makeshift reins, he prepared to strangle his prey. He braced his feet between the stair rails for support. Rechecking the rearview mirror, he steadied his death gripping hands. A rush of adrenaline courses through his veins as he pulled the ends with intense force, taking her life away. Nancy instantly succumbed to her death without a fight. Allan continued to aimlessly drive down the road bobbing to the tunes, totally unaware of what had taken place.

After driving silently for a while, Allan glanced over at Nancy. He noticed something was wrong with her. Reaching over he touched one of her stiff unresponsive hands. "Honey are you okay?" Allan reacted in a panicked voice quickly stopping to help her. Pulling over he released his seatbelt, then quickly forced the gearshift into park. He stood up rushing to assist his wife. The assailant grabbed the elderly man and forced him to the floor. Allan tried in vain to defend himself against his aggressor. The bloody brawl ended when the felon punched him in the temple rendering him useless. Before Allan could get back on his feet the stranger wrapped his hands around his neck and strangled him to death.

Nancy faded into thin air. I sat with my eyes closed waiting for the dizziness to pass. This reaction is similar to

coming out of a deep meditation. I waited for the phase to pass before heading home.

The following afternoon I headed west to do readings in a small community. Along the highway I noticed a billboard offering a reward for the missing couple.

"Mrs. Rogers, if I happen to drive by the location you're in could you please direct me," I asked out loud hoping she might hear me.

The area beyond the sign broke into a divided highway. Two lanes of traffic headed west. The middle was divided by a city block of dense forest. After this divide, two lanes headed east. I continued to drive the straight highway. Several kilometers ahead to my left I noticed a roadside grave. Two low flying crows almost struck my windshield, as they headed south. I wasn't going to jump to any conclusions over these possible signs. This wasn't concrete enough for me.

On the drive home, a magenta pink blur took over my left eye, slowing me down enough to miss two deer that leapt onto the highway. Fifty miles later, I slowed down while entering the questionable area. A flash of fuchsia pink lit up a specific wilderness area south of the highway. A sign at the side read: Dead End. I pulled over to the side of the road and slowly backed my car to the corner before turning down a gravel road. Crossing the bog, the rest of the area began to look extremely familiar. I needed to head home as dusk was starting to take. Being in the back bush alone can be very dangerous. I needed to bring someone back with me during daylight hours.

The following day I found a friend who was willing to go with me. We headed to the site together. Shortly after turning off the highway, I forced my low-riding PT Cruiser down a grassy trail.

The road was identical to the fallen "f" I had been previously shown. A slough of murky water lay south of the grassy trail. The raised circle on the map was a huge beaver dam. I could sense Mrs. Rogers nearby, but I needed time to work on this.

The scene made sense. He drove the RV in with dead bodies, stopped and submerged under the water beside the dam. Heavy ruts dented the grass trail, equivalent to those of a motor home turning around in the brush.

Driving into the closest village, I spotted a police car patrolling the area. I followed him block after block flashing my headlights in his rear view mirror. I'd brake behind him at a stop sign, honk my horn and unroll the window waving and gesturing to get his attention. Five blocks later, he finally pulled over. I rushed up to his cruiser. The young officer of approximately twenty eight sunk down on his front seat, looking at me like an innocent schoolboy through his rolled down window.

"Excuse me, Officer. Thank you for pulling over." I took a deep breath before carrying on.

"I understand you generally pull people over instead, but I really need to talk to you. I believe I know where the Rogers are. Could I show you? They're less than five minutes away," I suggested, hoping he would take me up on the offer.

"The case isn't open," immediately popped out his mouth. "Call the Crime Hotline, the number is displayed on the billboard."

"Why don't you take my name and number?"

"No, I can't. That would mean I'd have to write a report."
Nancy partially materialized beside the cop car.
Unfortunately she was only visible to me. If only he could
see her desperation.

"I'm sorry, but I need to carry on with my patrol."

I walked to my car, shaking my head in total disgust.
You'd think a rookie would want to help break a
prominent case. What a waste of tax dollars. I should have
taken his name and badge number, but what was the use?
His sergeant was probably no better. I resumed my
position back in the driver's seat in total silence. My
friend sat there busting a gut in laughter.

"I've never seen anyone pull over a cop before," she
laughed, sliding up the passenger seat.

"At least you had the thrill of seeing me in action, but that
chap was totally useless."

I called the hotline after a long drive home. A strong
intuitive feeling took over that this operator had no idea
about the case I was reporting.

"You seem unfamiliar with this situation. May I ask where
you're located?"

"I'm in New York," the operator replied.

"Can you put me through to a Canadian dispatcher?"

"I'm sorry, we just answer the line. Eventually the reports
end up with the right people." She seemed to somehow
have faith in the flawed system. "Oh, here's the number of
the constable who handles this case." The lady gave me

the number. Before hanging up, I obtained the case number as well.

I called the supplied number and left a message. A week later I received a call from an officer in northern Alberta. This officer's attitude was colder than the arctic.

"Who are the Rogers?" he asked in an arrogant tone. "What on earth are you talking about? I'm up in High Level, I've never heard of them." I had to start with him all over again on my costly daytime cell phone. "I'll pass this on to someone else who's better able to handle this." By the end of the conversation he was lost and I was spent. Getting to the proper people was going to be a challenge.

After this, I called the detachment that services the area involved, hoping for a better response. But I was quickly dismissed by the operator, who dished out a 1-800 number before hanging up. She supplied me with the same number I had started with.

"Good Heavens, what is it going to take to get them to listen," I muttered to myself, before getting back on the blower and calling her back. "I just called a few minutes ago about the Rogers. Can't you at least give me a local officer to speak with?" She put me on hold for a few minutes.

A friendly female voice answered the line. After sharing the information, the officer took my name and number. Weeks later I received a call from another officer from northern Alberta. We briefly went over the facts, before he sent the details to the triage unit. These are the people who decide which leads to follow. During our conversation, I discovered the team was over four hours away from the crime scene, and this officer was several hours away from them.

Weeks later I called this officer again to find out where things stood, only to be told that my lead didn't fit their protocol, so it had been put at the back of their file

"What do you mean, it doesn't fit?" I needed further clarification.

"They won't consider it. They don't take leads from psychics. You're probably good at what you do, but there are a lot of crackpots out there. I hope you don't take this personally. Perhaps in the future they'll reconsider your lead."

"Do you have a few moments? I have some questions."

"Sure, I have a few moments. What can I help you with?"

"Is it okay for me to dig around looking for them?" I needed to know exactly where I stood acting on my own.

"Yes, as long as you have permission from the land owner. What ever you do, don't trespass. Otherwise you could end up in trouble," warned the officer.

"Can any useful resources be lent, or trained personnel be sent out to us?"

"Unfortunately, we can't do that. Our resources are limited."

"Officer, I don't think you understand, but I don't have any resources. Can you ask triage if they'd be willing to entertain my lead one last time? Otherwise, next Tuesday a group of us will attempt to find them ourselves."

My friend Deb who was intuitively inclined assisted me in lining up people to help with the search for the Rogers. We had everything planned including the coffee break. We raided our garden sheds for hoes and rakes the night before. Our cars were packed and ready to hit the road first thing in the morning.

I was lying partially awake in bed on Tuesday morning. A film of visions crammed my third eye. Elongated letter "f;" in other words the map flashed. Then the number "25" was presented at the edge of the road. Three raised white ovals were numbered "1," "2" and "3." Number "2" was circled several times. I thanked my guide for the display. Sliding out of bed, I grabbed my cell phone and turned it on. In the blurred distance, I noticed my voicemail icon flashing. Wondering what someone needed that early in the morning drove me to retrieve the message.

"This is a message for Laura Laforce. This is an important call from the police department. It is 8 am September 28' 2011. In the event that you find the Rogers please don't disturb the crime scene. You must call the police should you find them. We appreciate your efforts. Call us if you need assistance or have further questions."

How dare the police stand at the sidelines refusing to help us. Protecting themselves by leaving authoritative messages is crap. I decided that if the couple was found that I'd be calling the media first.

I called Deb before I left the house. She received an identical message on her voicemail as well. We decided not to pick up any calls originating from the police department. My phone was already programmed with the number this call originated from. If they wanted to be included, they'd have to participate.

"Laura, what are we going to do if we find the Rogers?"

"Ah, invite them for supper," I answered with the most hilarious raspy tone I could possibly conjure.

"Laura!" Deb was instantly appalled by my unsolicited humor.

"Perhaps we'll call the media first and forget the little boy's club," I uttered in a mocking tone.

"I contacted their family last night." Disappointment surged through her tone.

"Did you get anywhere?"

"Not really, they're not allowed to accept information from the public. They have to turn over any leads directly to the police."

"I bet they have no idea how badly the case is being managed. Victims are often blinded by faith in the faulty system." I felt frustrated. "I was shown something this morning, but I'll wait until we're all there to share the details."

The group gathered in a circle and I shared the latest vision with them. We ascertained that the three ovals represented the three beaver dams. The number "25" was a measurement from the edge of the road. Twenty five yards led to dam number one and twenty five metres led to dam number two.

We quickly decided how to search the area. Each person grabbed a rake or hoe. I chose to create my own device, which comprised of a telescopic pole with a hooked tow rope secured to the end by duct tape.

"Everybody be careful, there's sewage in the water. You don't want to come down with beaver fever. It'll kill you," one of the fussy volunteers warned.

I didn't sense us being in any danger. I started wondering why the beavers were absent. This area should be packed with beavers, especially with three beaver dams in the vicinity. "Deb, did you notice there isn't a single beaver in sight. Don't you find that odd? This place has nothing but beaver ruts, runs and dams."

"I noticed that too. Apparently a cadaver in the water would cause beavers to vacate the pond. Remember when I started retching while pulling up the bailing twine?" Things were making sense.

"What was up with that?" Her response was unusual. I wondered if something flew into her mouth causing her to react so strongly.

"I was scared that I found one of the bodies. I figured he must have tied them up. I didn't know how I was going to handle things if we actually found them."

"I've felt that way myself many times, but when things happen, you'll find a way to cope," I reassured her.

Things were starting to add up. I became exhausted after dipping my search device into the water several times and retrieving logs. I took one step too close to the edge and my foot started to sink into the mud. Great, now what do I do? I gently tugged, trying to release my right foot which was stuck to the top of the ankle. Then the left foot started to gradually go under. Attempts to free my feet brought on intense abdominal spasms. I tried in vain to hold back my tears of pain. I was frustrated that I no longer had any sort of strength with being sick and weak.

I couldn't let the others see me this way. Sharp pains radiated from under my bottom left ribcage.

A volunteer firefighter rushed over to help me. "I want you to hold onto me, while I get you unstuck. I'm scared you're going to get hurt. You don't look well. You should be at home resting not out here in the wilderness searching for missing people." He released me from the mud hole within seconds. I thanked him for helping me.

"I'm a trained rescue professional. I can guarantee you were in this over your head. I don't know how to do this. We don't have the training or equipment to handle this. We need a vacuum truck, a cherry picker and a back hoe. If something like this was to happen at work, a specialized team would be called. Not enthusiastic housewives, who claim to have abilities and who bring an arsenal of garden rakes, hoes and homemade devices held together by duct tape."

"We do things this way, because the police won't help us. We've asked for help and equipment, but they keep refusing."

"Don't you think if they were here, we should have come across clothing or something by now? Do you still think they're here?" he asked, trying to reason with me.

"I understand your concern. It is very frustrating to find nothing right off the bat, but this isn't unusual either. It is like finding a needle in the haystack. It's never an easy endeavor."

The group briefly broke for coffee and gathered around one of the vans.

"Hey, you guys. Look at Laura. Something is seriously wrong with her. Her lips are turning blue." Beaver Fever lady was on my case, frantically voicing her concern for me. "Her heart isn't pumping enough oxygen."

I climbed into one of the running vehicles to warm up. Feeling under the weather, I should have been home resting,

Instead of out looking for bodies. I closed my eyes and quietly asked my spirit guide to give me a sign that I'm going to be okay. I instantly received an "F" for fine. I went on to ask if we were going to find the Rogers and "O" appeared.

I couldn't sit back and have the others relentlessly searching. It was time to call off the search. Dragging my poor body out of the sanctuary of the warm vehicle, I reunited with the search party. One volunteer was preoccupied with dousing with a pendulum. Another lady repeatedly struck her Himalayan chime bowl, seeking direction. I couldn't understand why they needed these items, but who was I to judge?

One of the young gals skipped up the trail swirling a pair of blue men's underwear on top of a branch. Once she got closer she started loudly singing. "I've got a dead man's underwear."

Right away, I joined in the fun and started an auction. "Ghostly Gonch to the highest bidder, one million dollars, do I hear a million?" Deb popped up her hand.

"Two million, do I hear two million?" Barb, a young mother, held up muddy sludge on the end of a stick from the slough.

"Miscellaneous ghost-wear goes to Barb, the mud master." The young gal randomly flung the underwear toward the winner. It took off like a kite in the wind before plummeting towards the ground landing on Barb's foot. A high pitched shriek penetrated the air as she accidentally kicked it into the pond. The laughter broke the tension.

"I appreciate everyone coming out today and I thank you for your help. I feel it's in our best interest to call off this search." I addressed the group.

"We don't have the equipment or expertise to handle this."

On the way home my cell phone rang: "Hi Laura. It's Heather. I'm calling to see if you're okay," she asked in a concerned tone.

"I've been watching you search filthy water looking a little frazzled. I see beaver dams and tall yellow clusters of grass and mud surrounding you."

"Don't worry about me. I'm fine. We were out searching for the Rogers. You know the missing couple?"

"That makes sense. I kept picking up your distress."

"You were probably picking up my physical pain and my frustration. I can see a golden outline of their bodies. Nancy is curled in the fetal position under the dam and Allan is close by."

"Eventually your lead will become valid. Sometimes we have to stand back and let others do the work. Please take care of yourself. I'm worried about you."

"Thanks, I will," I reassured her before hanging up.

Months later a man with authority showed up at my door. He wanted to know if I knew where the Rogers were. The expression on my face was probably a dead giveaway. I grabbed my paper pad and wrote out all the details and directions. I carefully went over them one by one with him. Ushering him to my office, I gave him photos of the area.

"This makes sense. I know the area. A search would be relatively easy with the right people and equipment." His face beamed. "I'm going to put a bug in some ears." He shook my hand thanking me and rushed out the door back into the blizzard outside.

I heard through the grapevine that this man passed the information onto a very capable detective in the area, who sent it back to the triage unit.

When I first encountered Nancy Rogers she was stuck in between. Earthbound Nancy kept reappearing as a ghost. She was irritated, endlessly searching for her beloved husband. It was bad enough she was murdered, but being unable to find Allan was unbearable. Other mediums assumed they were buried apart. Through communication with my spirit guides I was able to ascertain that she was stuck and he crossed over. With being in two different dimensions they were unable to find each other. Once I started writing her story she crossed over to the other side.

Allan Rogers crossed over at the moment of his death, refusing to appear to me until earlier today. Oddly enough, both the orbs containing the souls of Nancy and Allan Rogers appeared one at a time, as I wrote up each of their murders. They hovered within two inches of the computer monitor. Nancy's orb was white and Allan's indigo blue. They were making sure the events of the crime were written accurately. Both resurfaced together at the end of their story. Before my eyes, the loving soul mates embraced each other and shared a romantic kiss, then disappeared from sight.

Efforts to find the couple have been extremely difficult. The hotline advertised on the billboard is answered in the United States, yet the crime took place in Canada. The reporting officer who supplies information to the team is six hours away from the murder scene. I've repeatedly attempted to present my reports to the team. The forensic triage unit working this particular case continually refuses to work with us.

Apparently my leads, for some absurd reason, don't fit the protocol. From what I've been given to understand, their focus is on an area five miles away. We volunteered our time and energy, without resources. From what we've been told the triage is working behind the scene, which I highly doubt. Over a year has gone by without any progress on their side.

Months later, I received a call from the intake officer who screens the calls. His name showed up on my call display. I answered the phone without greeting him by name. He was uncomfortable, hesitant and searching for words. Seconds later he claimed to have the wrong number and hung up. I haven't heard from him since.

Fortunately, not all detachments handle cases this way. Good officers and capable investigators are out there resolving crime.

I sat across from TJ at a restaurant in northern Alberta. I made several unsuccessful attempts to call home to check on my resistant teenager, who chose to stay home. The phone was never picked up, after dialing home several times. A few minutes later, the voice mail icon appeared in my cell's display. I rushed to access the message.

"Hi Laura, this is Constable Steve, calling on behalf of the RCMP. Could you please call me ASAP." My heart leapt into my throat, as panic mode set in. I hung up the phone in a frazzled state. I was so tense that I couldn't read or concentrate on the menu. I slammed it shut and slid it towards TJ. Right at that moment the waitress showed up at the table ready to take our order.

"TJ, order something for me. I just can't right now," I demanded almost falling to pieces.

"Can we have a few more minutes? We're not ready to order yet." TJ politely smiled, attempting to save the day.

"What's wrong Laura? You were fine two minutes ago."

"I can't get a hold of Mary. She's not answering the phone or answering texts. I'm worried sick about her. Plus, I just received a message from a Mountie asking me to call right away." I was a wreck. My hands were shaking. I needed to quickly contain myself.

"Did you see or sense anything bad happening?"

"No, but I received a vision this morning all lit up in gold. A golden crown was revealed on a label or badge. Two golden hands exchanged a hand shake."

"Laura, I bet this call is about one of your cold cases and nothing to do with Mary." TJ gently massaged my quivering hands from across the table.

I quickly dialed the number supplied by the cop. "Good evening, Beaver County Detachment. How may I direct your call?"

This detachment was several hours away from my home. With a sigh of relief, I asked to speak with Constable Steve. The operator put me through and a man's voice answered.

"Hi Constable Steve, I'm Laura Laforce, I understand you wanted to speak to me."

"Yes, I called you several hours ago. I'm looking into the cold case of Nicole Isabelle. I understand you might be able to provide us with some details."

"Yes, I do have information for you."

"Is it true that you're a medium and that you communicate with the dead?" he quizzed me, trying to understand.

"Yes, Officer."

"Are you willing to come down to the station and do a taped video interview?"

"Yes."

An appointment was set for the following week. After being postponed several times, the interview finally took place. Two years had passed since I'd communicated with Nicole's ghost. This matter was reported to the police two years earlier. I never thought this day would arrive.

Sitting in the police station, my only inhibition was being on camera. I lacked confidence in my physical appearance. Knowing that I'd probably never see the filmed interview was a personal relief.

The officer invited me into his corporal's office to go over the details. I sat in a comfortable padded office chair across the desk from him. The previously dread of being filmed was no longer a big deal.

A huge bag of nutty trail mix resting a few feet away from my face, literally threatened my safety. Being deathly allergic to nuts, I felt uneasy. I sat silently, wondering if the bag had been recently opened. I contemplated asking the cop to remove them. If he accidentally disturbed loose allergens, I would have been in big trouble. I faced a bigger problem; my epi-pen was expired. I felt like excusing myself from the room. I calmed myself down and quietly asked Spirit if I'd be okay.

"Yes" was written in huge letters on the wall behind the officer.

"What information do you have in regards to Nicole's whereabouts?" The constable's pleasant smile helped to ease my unrelated stress.

"I'm a medium. Late one evening, I was visiting with one of my clients. While having tea, I sensed an entity with us. This was when the client asked if I could locate a missing woman. I started tapping into the ghost's energy. I could see a shadow of a heavy woman lurking along the living room wall wearing heavy winter clothing with rollers in her hair. Nicole was lured from her home by a strange man looking for directions. She left her home peacefully without a struggle."

"How do you know he was looking for directions?" the officer quizzed, looking quite intent.

"A map is revealed, but keep in mind that the dead usually communicate through symbolism."

"Did you see her get into a vehicle?"

"No, I vaguely remember seeing a running vehicle outside of her house. I can only make out dense clouds of exhaust fumes. I'm only shown things that are significant."

"Then what happened?" he asked, waiting to hear the rest.

"I was shown a small bridge with a pipe-shaped stream underneath, which veered east. She kept flashing N for north and 5 for distance. I thought it was odd for a bridge to be in a rural area. After sharing this with my client, she brought me out to see it."

"Did you know there are other bridges around here?" he questioned with a sincere look on his face.

"Not that I'm aware of. I'm not from here. I don't know the area. I know that bridge is the correct one, because everything out there matches everything I saw."

"What matches?" He started to push for concrete evidence.

"The bridge has wooden guard rails. A narrow stream runs east of the bridge. There is a substantial curve in the land. This is the point where the killer buried her. Specific fence posts mark the entrance to the crime scene. These posts also line up with her body."

"Why do these fence posts stand out?"

"I was shown a series of three different fence posts. One skinny rebar slanted right, another of heavy metal triple the thickness, which stood upright. The third is wooden and slanted left. A major point of interest is pointed out between the second and the third poles. These line up with her grave, which is down half a block at the crest. Her body lies approximately eight feet from the top of the bank north of the creek. She is lying east to west and her body is buried at hip level."

"Did you know how she was killed?"

"She was struck in the head by a huge five pound, oval shaped rock."

"Did you see the guy kill her?"

Nicole tried to get away. She was running in snow on the bank just past the bridge. Her assailant grabbed her with his free arm and struck the back of her head with a heavy stone that he gripped in his other hand.

"The stranger who killed her was a Caucasian male in his late forties to mid-fifties. His hair was a whitish blonde. Brush cut like yours only shorter. He was very muscular and stood approximately six foot. He has since expired, but I can identify him through photos. I don't have a name for you."

"How do you know she was buried?"

"The suspect I described was standing above a shallow open grave facing the crest. He dumped a white powdered substance over her out of a fifty pound white bag. Two corners of the bag are bunched together."

"Was there any writing on the bag?" The cop asked.

"None, just a plain white cloth-like bag. I don't know what the substance is that he poured on top of her."

"How do you know how deep the grave is?"

"The depth was measured up to the hips of a black spiritual stickman figure standing in the grave. To me I find the depth factual. Over a year ago I dug down in the area and reached water at hip level."

"Was anyone else involved?"

"There is a man still alive. He is either directly or indirectly involved, but he is definitely aware of her murder. This man was approximately thirty eight at the time of the incident. He has dark hair, a heavy moustache, a round face and tanned skin."

"Does anyone else know about this?"

"Yes." I must have blushed a million shades of red.

"Who else knows?" I must have taken my interviewer by surprise with my reaction.

"Thousands," I answered. "Anyone who read my book knows. I got frustrated and wrote it up. All names and locations have been changed. Therefore the situation can remain anonymous.

"You're an author?" He met my gaze with total shock.

"Yes."

"Is there anything else that comes to you?"

"Yes, I understand she went missing in the winter. What throws me off slightly is the burial seems to take place in the spring. The grass is yellow, which doesn't fit. There could be only three possible reasons for this. The first reason would be a brown winter. I've never taken time to research the weather back then. The second situation could be that she was stored during the winter and buried after the ground thawed. The last explanation I have for this is for me to be able to see the area and the killer without a heavy covering of snow or winter clothing. I have had the last scenario occur many times before. It helps better describe the area and pertinent landmarks. If I saw the entire scene in snow, I wouldn't have recognized the creek or the distance from the bank."

"Would you mind accompanying me to the site? That way I can mark down the co-ordinates required to further investigate this case."

"Yes, I have some time. I have clients booked to see me at one o'clock."

"I'll take you through the shortcut and you'll have plenty of time." The officer quickly glanced at his wrist watch.

We bundled up in winter gear and headed out to the rural bridge. I immediately walked towards the mixed fence posts with the officer in the howling wind.

"See these posts?" This is exactly what I was shown. If you look between the second and third post, these almost draw a straight line to Nicole's remains at the crest."

"It's unreal how all of this is matching up. All the physical descriptions are right before our eyes." The officer's eyes lit up in total amazement.

"Do you want to go to her grave area?"

"Yes, let's go!"

I rushed towards the barbed wire fence looking for the perfect entrance.

"You don't have to go through there. We have access through the gate. The farmer opened it for us earlier today."

Walking beside him I noticed the badge on his sleeve. A royal crown sat at the curved peak. Finally the message I received up north with a golden crowned emblem and handshake made sense. Golden messages are always good, but sometimes things take time to manifest.

"I heard another medium claims that Nicole's body is under a tire nailed to plywood. This is something that I haven't been shown. I've never seen it."

The officer pointed towards the middle of the field closer to the tree line. "It's over there."

I focused to see it and stumbled briefly lost my footing on the uneven icy ground.

"Watch your step, it's very slick out here," he warned, as we headed into the chilling wind.

We walked directly to the article. "I don't know what this is, but Nicole isn't under there. I can't understand why this other medium insists she's under the marker. She is buried closer to the bank. I have no feeling here."

"It's a cattle feed," he announced, cluing me in.

To me it looked a little small for cows to be eating out of, but why would he lie to me? Perhaps something else goes on top of the circular tire, but again, I didn't know. We walked toward the bank in the vicious wind. I could sense frostbite licking at my earlobes. A warm toque would have been a smart choice. Underneath my feet bubbled with a sudden burst of energy.

"This is the spot where Nicole is buried."

The officer started marking the coordinates, took some pictures and jotted down some notes. Chilled to the bone, we headed back to the vehicles that were parked at the bridge.

"I really appreciate you coming out. I'm going to get the paperwork in so that an investigation can be started. This area is small and the information seems to be valid."

"Are they going to dig up the area?" I inquired slightly curious about the next step.

"No, we bring in a company who uses sonar radar. Their equipment is capable of finding bodies buried underground."

"Oh."

"Well, thank you for your time," he extended a handshake.

"Here's my card. Do you have a business card?" I grabbed one out of my pocket and handed it over. "Follow me out. I'll get you back to town in time for your appointments."

The police officer led the way to the motel that I'd be working out of. I arrived several minutes before the first reading was to start. I spent the remainder of the day working with the locals.

In my opinion, police departments should be more open and willing to working with mediums. It was a privilege to be able to assist this detachment in their cold case. Being open I receive invaluable information from the beyond on a regular basis. It's hard to walk around knowing exactly what has taken place, and most times being unable to do anything with this pertinent information.

Chapter 4

Breach of Competence

It is my opinion that we no longer have a capable system of rendering justice. We desperately need changes. Judges should be chosen and governed by the public. They need to be held legally accountable for any negligence transpired.

The telephone rang disturbing my morning meditation. "Hi Laura, this is Brenda. I'm the attorney you recently helped. I need your assistance again. Is there anyway you could squeeze me in tonight. I have a desperate situation and court in the morning with the judge from hell."

Within the hour, Brenda was sitting across from me.

"Laura I have a terrible situation going on. I know what I'm up against and I need support. Do you believe in evil?"

"Yes."

"How can one person be so twisted that they literally destroy the lives around them?"

I shut my eyes and could see a dark entity behind bars. The number "22" revealed his total convictions. Flashes of his past activities were presented. I was shown him spitting on Brenda when she turned to leave his pen. Spirit labeled his expelled spittle as "HIV". His forte was burglary and assault. He severely beat an elderly store clerk rendering him unconscious. A black and white premonition revealed a young lady resembling Brenda, lying limp in a pool of blood in the middle of a street.

"This convict you're dealing with is extremely evil. His energy is pitch black. He must remain jailed in order for society to be safe. He spit on the side of your face when you left his cell."

"How did you know?"

"I was shown what happened. Not only is he violent, but he's also sick."

"Yeah, he's sick in the head alright."

No listen to me. His aura exhibits that he's HIV positive. Be careful. You're at risk when dealing with him. Request that he's to wear a spit guard before you see him or have a plexiglass divider separating you from his bodily fluids. You're okay, but please don't put yourself at further risk. He almost killed an elderly gentleman during a robbery. He's rotten to the core."

"This judge I'm dealing with is a conceited selfish bastard. His only concern is clearing the courtroom to go golfing."

"Even though you have concrete evidence this case will be minimized. The judge will dish out community service. This criminal will be released immediately." I could see a black number two written on the wall behind the attorney. Then the word "sister" appeared shortly after.

"Brenda, within two months, your twin sister's life will be at risk. He is going to mistake her for you."

Brenda's jaw popped open. Total shock embraced her entire aura. "How did you know about my twin sister?"

"The woman lying on the road resembles you, but her nose is slightly different."

"Laura you're scaring me. I do have an identical twin sister. When she was five she broke her nose on the edge of the sandbox. She has a permanent bend on the bridge of her nose. Are you telling me he's going to kill my sister?"

"He's going to harm her." "Can this be stopped?"

"Not unless he's locked up. This is more than a warning. If things are drawn out in black and white they can usually be altered. I didn't see a coffin, but a motionless body."

Tension penetrated the air. I closed my eyes and connected with her guide again. "Is the judge going to lock up this dangerous villain?"

The letter "X" meaning "no" was instantly revealed from beyond. I could see a robed figure with a gavel in his hand. He was slumped over his pulpit and grasping his chest. An image of a solid black quivering heart appeared right beside him.

"Brenda there are going to be problems with this case. The convict you're dealing with is extremely dangerous. This district judge isn't capable of handling this situation. I do see another judge taking over shortly."

"Oh no, you don't understand. These county judges don't quit. They die or retire."

"I've been shown the judge is going to suffer a major heart attack. All you need to do is buy time. This is your only hope of locking this convict away."

The attorney postponed her case the following morning. Four days later the judge suffered a massive heart attack. He flat lined in his courtroom. Extensive efforts were made to revive him, but his soul refused to return.

The case was heard several weeks later with a new judge. He sentenced the brutal criminal to fifteen years with no chance for parole.

Weeks later a hysterical woman's voice frantically squealed over the phone line.

"I need to see someone. Can I come see you right now?"

An hour later, she arrived and took a seat across from me at the kitchen table. Her bloodshot eyes filled with tears before the session had even started. Her body quivered with anxiety as she tried to keep herself together.

I closed my eyes to connect with her guide to catch a glimpse of her situation. Scenes of domestic violence played out before my third eye. Her ex-husband was a very violent man. His only intention was to kill her. She needed to run for her life. She needed to protect her three young children.

"You're in danger and so are your children. Your husband is trying to kill you. Your place is going to be under attack tonight. You must not return. Do you understand?"

"Help me. I'm scared. I can't do this alone. His lawyer says I'm not allowed to move."

"I know that you are scared, but I need you to be brave. He is going to have you killed if you go home tonight. He's after you."

"You don't understand. He's a very bad man. He hurts the children and the courts want him to have visits. Last week he molested our son in the middle of the night when I was sleeping. He recently punched my youngest son in the stomach. His lawyer said it was my fault that I didn't protect my son from this."

"I do understand what you're going through. I'm on your side. None of this is going to be easy. I've been through this myself. My ex had attempted to kill me numerous times. I almost lost my life due to the stupidity of the courts," I said.

"My situation is worse. Uniformed guards hired by the woman's shelter accompanied me to court yesterday from my apartment. One sat on each side of me and another two across the room. After court was over they brought me home and patrolled inside and outside the building. I heard there was a similar case about six years ago."

"That would have been my case," I calmly stated realizing how far I'd come.

"In my case there are three lawyers. I have one, my ex has one and our three children share one. Our hearing yesterday was a very disheartening nightmare. It all started off when the judge uttered 'Oh Triage' in a mocking manner as the lawyers approached the bench. The three of them giggled with the judge and exchanged looks before starting my case."

"The judge immediately downgraded my desperate situation in his courtroom. He ordered me to meet up with my ex-husband at 10:00 am December 25th in the West River Park Mall parking lot. Then he smirked and smugly stated, 'It will be an interesting to see the two of you getting along in a vacant parking lot on Christmas morning with no one around.' Then the judge turns around and speaks to my ex like he's some sort of victim telling him that he may take the children unsupervised to the Yukon for Christmas."

"The guards protecting me were appalled. I was devastated and broke down bawling like a baby. She had no interest in the fact he'd already been sexually inappropriate with his son. The judge neglected to consider his huge stack of criminal records involving theft, assault, drinking and driving, and possession of narcotics. My lawyer tried bringing this up and was immediately shut down by the judge. This judge threatened to send me to jail, if I didn't hand the children over."

"I understand. Your situation is almost identical to mine including the ludicrous remarks. You don't have to meet him alone." I shut my eyes and I was shown a telephone, the mall, security and a cop's badge.

"You need to call mall security. They work around the clock 24/7. You're going to be on their property and he'sviolent towards you." I felt badly for her. It wasn't too long ago I'd been there myself. I could feel tears welling up in my eyes and fought them back. She was being victimized by the system. There was no way out of the corner she'd been backed into.

"I wish I was strong like you."

"There was a time that I was just like you. I've grown through experience. I wasn't always strong. I spent hours sick with fear. I ran for my life. I prayed for survival. Even when you're scared you can't let the fear take over."

"You're okay?"

"Yes, I'm fine. Let's get back to you. Your ex-husband has lied about you. His lawyer is unethical. He is unable to filter fact from fiction. His lawyer has convinced your lawyer that you're a crazy liar. The horrific events you've shared with your lawyer are being used against you. They have already judged the situation and nobody is going to listen."

"I have a restraining order, but last night Richard threw a large fist-sized rock through my kitchen window. I called 911 and many hours later the cops arrived. I was told it was neighborhood kids and that I was overreacting."

I closed my eyes and immediately I was shown her ex-husband Richard was behind this. She was doing dishes when the rock sailed through the kitchen pane and landed beside her foot.

"Richard was responsible last night. He threw it himself. You were doing dishes when it landed at your feet. Broken glass shattered everywhere."

"How did you know? I didn't tell you the whole story."

"You didn't have to. Your spirit guide did. Be careful when you're dealing with the police. Make sure they listen to you. And if they won't, go over their heads to the person above them. Cops don't understand domestic violence nor do they like dealing with it. Your life is in jeopardy and you are going to need their help. Try to see if you can get a spousal violence team who specializes in these situations assigned to your case."

"I'm afraid of my husband having the children alone. He drives under the influence of alcohol and drugs. Last week my son Jason called me from his father's house to tell me his father was driving drunk and pulling over to puke. His Dad hit a curb and a guardrail before deciding to return home. Hearing this, I called the police. They asked me to call them if he was still drunk that evening when I picked the children up. I told them I couldn't because of his history of violence with me. The police suggested I ask someone else to go up to his vehicle and see if he's drunk. I can't believe the danger my children are forced to face."

"I hear you." I replied trying to contain my fury in order to help my client. They won't deal with this unless they to catch him in the act."

"The last time my ex picked them up in a borrowed vehicle with no seatbelts. He took them from the pickup point to see their court appointed child psychologist. My boys kept complaining to their therapist about having no seat belts and facing a highway trip home. He completely ignored them, refusing to help them out. After their appointment, he sent them out to face an icy winter highway, without proper restraints. I found out about this after the fact. I was livid and called the police. Apparently it's not illegal to drive in vehicles without seatbelts if there aren't any. The drinking and driving is still illegal and the cops aren't doing a thing," she explained almost falling to pieces.

"Yes, that's right. But with the domestic calls you've already made, they'll minimize any future complaints.

They won't react to you the same. Your chances of receiving help are limited. I know; I've been there. I'm sorry, but this is what you're up against." I warned my desperate client who sat across from me.

"I complained to Social Services and they refused to investigate, because a custody battle was going on."

"I hear you loud and clear. Society has fallen and they don't dare interfere."

"Does my life get better or am I always going to be looking over my shoulder?"

"In about a year the worst will be over. Then you'll be able to start building the life you initially wanted. You sacrificed your own needs serving him. You applied to go to university. You were accepted into the commerce program. He was against you having the education and forced you to drop out."

"How did you know that?"

"I was shown the forms, the written acceptance and you standing in tears, shredding the documents."

"Why is it that he chases me and torments me?"

"This is called ownership. It's a sick type of control. This will gradually lessen as time goes on."

"He keeps threatening to kill me. Do I need to worry?"

I shut my eyes and went to Spirit. "He's going to make a couple of more attempts, but he doesn't injure you. You're going to be aware of things before they happen. You know the feelings you've been having lately before he shows up unannounced at the door?"

"Yes, I'm surprised you know that."

"You're being guided to safety by your spirit guide through your intuition. You need to pay attention to any warnings you receive. You'll know what to do."

"Do you see me buying the place I'm staying at?"

A vision of a moving van was revealed followed by a number "3."

"No, I see you moving another three times."

"You don't understand. I like this house."

"I hear you, but that's not what's in store for you."

I bumped into her a year later. She went back to school. Her divorce came through. The ex was no longer a threat. He even stopped seeing the children. She was pleased to announce her third move to a brand new house of her own.

Judicial government systems are tainted with corruption. Judges lack the ability to diligently make decisions. Criminals and their lawyers run the show impairing the system. Innocent people are victimized by these antics. They pay enormous sums to be legally assisted, resulting in being legally assaulted.

Chapter 5

Core Corruption

Our world is in crisis. Most governments are corrupt. Both inside and outside influences with hidden agendas taint today's leaders. The leaders act like puppets, publicly delivering decisions from their party, even if they don't agree. Values and ethical codes of conduct no longer exist. Greed and hostility now rule. Death threats are uttered to those who are capable of exposing their hidden secrets.

On April Fool's Day, I received an invitation to attend a local political forum; "Choose Responsible Government."

What a joke. I muttered to myself. The masters of corruption and deceit, they'll shake your hand and rob you blind. They nod and smile, then spit in your face. They promise the world, then empty your wallets leaving you stranded. We're so preoccupied trying to survive, many don't notice their tactics until it's too late.

I sat wondering why people would attend such a useless mundane event. If it hadn't been for my curiosity, I would have probably stayed home. I arrived shortly before the main speaker was to address the crowd.

"Excuse me! Our voting system isn't fair. Ridings are elected and not the people. Each vote should represent the person of choice," interrupted a loud woman's voice from the back.

"She's right!" I butted in, unable to contain myself."Different politicians alter and manipulate the process, making it unfair. We are sick of being controlled by political parties who cheat. The voting has become fixed and very dishonest. Our ballots only have a list of certain choices. The public aren't able to select 'none of the above.' Many of us have stopped voting because of the dishonesty. Perhaps we should all stop paying our taxes, so our hard earned money doesn't get wasted on this bullshit. I know I could find millions of better things to put my money on."

My last statement brought on a standing ovation.

After the meeting was adjourned, the lady who complained about the voting came towards me and introduced herself. Other people from the crowd stopped by to talk and the politicians avoided us like the plague.

The following morning, I received a call from stranger. "I've been receiving death threats lately." She spoke in an anxious voice.

"Can you tell me what you see?"

"You're a politician. These threats are real. They know you're onto them. They're trying to keep you quiet. You're going to have to watch your back."

I allowed myself time to channel her spirit guide. I needed verification that she was going to be alright.

"Please give me a sign that I can understand." Her silhouette was shown to me by Spirit. The energy surrounding her beamed a bright yellow. 'Are these associates going to hurt her?' I continue. "0" was drawn in midair by her guide meaning "no."

"Is my life at risk?" The lady panicked, waiting for my reply.

"These guys mean business, but Spirit won't let them touch you. It's not in your contract," I told her.

"How do you know?" she demanded in a hostile tone.

"The energy in your aura is fine. Your spirit guide verified that you wouldn't be harmed."

"What does that have to do with possibly being murdered?" she argued.

"We all have life contracts. The energy of our souls changes before departing. It doesn't matter what the cause of death is going to be."

"So are you telling me that I'm safe?"

"Yes."

"Can you tell me who's behind all of this? We had another threatening call this morning at the office. Yesterday my secretary found a bug in her office."

"There's a tall, heavy set, dark haired, Italian male with a full beard and moustache. He's approximately fifty-two years of age. His name starts with an "F." This man smokes chubby cigars and is constantly clearing his throat. He works down the hall from you and he has ties with the mafia."

There was a gasp on the other side as she freaked. "Oh my God, that's Frankie. I thought the man respected me. He's always quiet around me."

"It's the silent types you need to be leery of," I warned her.

"He's had some dishonest dealings lately. He knows you caught wind of this. A blonde haired female approximately twenty-five years of age employed by you is his informant. You've got an outsider with the access of an insider." The politician thanked me for my time before hanging up the phone.

Corruption runs through many levels of government and big businesses as well.

A client who was a banker came in to see me. He sat across the table and started explaining his story:

"Weeks ago there was an argument over a high end investment account with my superiors. My boss called me into his office for a meeting after work. On my way out the door his assistant sucker punched me. I spun around and decked him in self defense.

"We ended up in a major fist fight in the huge office area right outside his door. We ferociously fought amongst the empty desks and ended up rolling on the floor. The fight ended when I punched the assistant in the face, breaking his nose.'

"After the brawl ended I pulled myself together and called the police. I was ready to press criminal charges on him for assault, when this bastard started trying to pin things on me. I still need to finish ironing out the details on this with the police. I haven't heard from them in the past two weeks. The attending officer said he'd be getting back to me."

"You won't be hearing from the police on this case. In their books the case is closed. 'I'll get back to you' is equivalent to 'not interested.' Going to the police isn't going to help. These people are protected through association. The cops won't believe you."

"I haven't gone back to work since this happened. Do you see me being able to get another job in this industry?"

"Yes, you'll be able to get work in another city. I know you're worried, but this is a situation that will never be mentioned." He thanked me for helping him, before he went on his way.

The moment he walked out the door a desperate man phoned.

"I don't want a reading. I need someone sensible to talk to who isn't connected to the government, healthcare or the oilfield. Can I make an appointment to see you? Would it be possible to see you today?"

An hour later he showed up at the door. The man was weak, exhausted and debilitated. My heart went out to him as I introduced myself.

He sat across from me explaining his situation.

"I'm an oilfield worker. I was injured in an accidental gas explosion at work last year. Two of my co-workers died. One died immediately and the other died in hospital the same day. I was rushed to the hospital clinging to life." He sat winded, coughing and sputtering and trying to catch his breath.

"I was in intensive care and on life support for several weeks. Two weeks after I was released, I had an aneurysm and spent another week in the hospital." Again he sat struggling to breathe. "My lungs haven't fully recovered. I can't walk across a room, speak or climb a few stairs without being winded."

"I'm sorry this happened to you," I sympathized with him.

"My employer and the government are trying to take away my disability. They send me to their doctors who are siding with them. These doctors won't listen to me. I was a healthy man before this happened."

These people are attempting to blame my medical condition on other illnesses. They've run a variety of tests on me trying to find other excuses. I've been tested for asthma, COPD, and many other things, including HIV." He sat gasping at the air for a minute.

"When the results came back normal they referred me to their psychiatrist. This doctor labeled me an unstable lazy manic depressive with hypochondriac tendencies."

I believed this worker 100 per cent, but needed guidance. I shut my eyes and silently asked his spirit guide for help.

I received a series of monochrome visual displays pertaining to his situation. "You need to avoid these people, especially the one with the white beard and the receding hairline. Be very careful around these medical professionals."

"Should I go to the College of Physicians and Surgeons?" He inquired with a poker straight face.

"No they're political; they'll side with the doctors," I warned him. Agencies funded by the taxpayers' dollars refuse to help and protect us.

"What about a top criminal lawyer?" he questioned.

"Most won't touch this because of those involved. There is one who will, but he will steal your money. He will smile to your face, then secretly take monetary bribes behind your back from them. You will be left exhausted and penniless. I know it's going to be difficult, but you need to find a third medical opinion. You need to also find a reliable trustworthy psychiatrist to reassess your situation."

"My family doctor believes me," he snapped.

"Yes, but you need one more who agrees with your physician's findings."

"Why would you want me to see another shrink?" He raised his voice with a concerned look on his face.

"Do you think I'm crazy?"

"No, you're sane and completely normal. You need to do this to gain a conflicting psychological report."

"Oh, I see," he replied in a relieved tone.

"Only address your lung situation and the tragic deaths of your two friends. Tell the doctor how you keep seeing your co-workers dying. Work this conversation to benefit you. You'll be granted permanent disability on the grounds of post-traumatic stress syndrome."

"Who would you suggest?"

I grabbed the phonebook and flipped through the directory. I found the physicians' page. Putting my finger at the top of the column, I shut my eyes. Spirit gently guided my finger down the column and stopped at Dr. Smith.

"Is this the correct person to assist him?" I asked.

A white flash dashed across the room, which verified the answer was "yes."

"Dr. Smith is the person to see," I said.

"Did you know oil refineries falsely mislead the public about safety concerns? These bigwigs lie about the dangers of living close to these plants. They boast about their emergency procedures, failing to mention that these will only be useful if the safety supervisors survive the disaster," he informed me.

"I've been very aware of this for years. A long time ago I was asked to attend a group survey. When I arrived, questions were asked about how safe we would feel living beside chemical factories. I started exposing hidden dangers they were trying to conceal. An official who'd been sitting behind an observation window made a hasty entry. He nervously approached me with cash in his hands. This man handed me a crisp fifty dollar bill and asked me to leave. He escorted me out of the interview room."

"Did you leave?" he gasped.

"Yes, I wasn't given the opportunity to stay. Unfortunately, these giant corporations don't care about the casualties. They brush off victims like debris, refusing to compensate them. These huge corporations end up having hugeprofits.

They pass on lucrative dividends to their wealthy investors instead."

"So these industrial monsters make me suffer. Then they turn around and pay big names like the Vatican and Queen instead," he quoted in an outrageous angry mocking manner.

"Yes, you're absolutely right."

"Does the Vatican really have an interest in our oilfield?" A look of total shock entered his face.

"Over twenty years ago, I did some temporary work in the Government Oils Division. One afternoon I was volunteered to help in the filing room. The lady in charge left me unattended. This is when I came across these particular files in my stack of documents to be filed. Being young and curious, I took the liberty to read through them.

"Around the same time, I was ordered to attend a staff meeting led by officials in the industry. Halfway during the session, dishonest double standards were presented to the employees in attendance. The presentation caught me by surprise. The visiting speaker mentioned that when an oil well owned by the crown is accidentally accessed by an unauthorized party a monetary fine will be delivered. Then he went on to mention that if the government should happen to tap into a private well, no compensation will be given to the owner of the well. This is when I raised my hand to address the speaker.

"The speaker looked slightly annoyed that I had the audacity to interrupt his session. Then he allowed me to question him. 'Why are you being dishonest with the public? Don't you believe in equality? Bullies operate this

way.' I wasn't done with him yet, when my boss's voice broke the tension in the room and ordered me to meet him in his office.

"I quickly popped out of my chair to leave the meeting. Peering around the room, I could see the faces of my stunned peers. Dead silence filled the room as I took my grand exit.

"A week earlier, a couple of co-workers had approached me. They complained that I took my work too seriously. They didn't want to go through another box of files before the weekend. One offered to buy me a book and a coffee. The other told me to go for a walk around the block.

"I excelled in finding wealthy people who hadn't bothered to pay taxes on oil wells. Finding these people was like a sport for me. I found more people in three months than this team did in five years. I didn't realize the others didn't share the same enthusiasm. This is when I was volunteered by them to help out in the filing room, where these files existed."

"What happened with the boss?" my client asked, straightening his stiff back against the chair.

"My boss eventually caught up with me in his office. He didn't appreciate my conduct at the staff meeting. He passed me a note pad and a pen, requesting that I write the official an apology. I sat for a few minutes deep in thought. I picked up the pen and scribed my leaving notice instead."

"You sure have balls. I wish I had your strength."

"I never used to view it that way. I always encountered situations as lessons to be learned from."

"Nobody can stop these huge corporations or the government," my client uttered in total despair.

"Unfortunately that's what many citizens think," I responded.

"There is going to be a time when the people will revolt against them."

"We Canadians are so laid back," he went on trying to comprehend this.

"Victims may be beaten several times during their lives. Once they've had enough, some of them eventually slap back. Today's youth are not going to tolerate this from those in authority."

"I'll give you that one," he replied, with a smile on his face.

"Remember the hockey game in Vancouver where losing brought on a riot? It will be along the same lines only worse, because they'll have the support of many around them. This type of upheaval will strike worldwide. The police will walk the perimeter of the attacks, but they'll be rendered powerless."

He thanked me for my help and drove past my husband on the way out the driveway. TJ strutted through the door moments later.

"You keeping the guys company?" He searched my face in a joking manner.

"All the time. Someone has to. It might as well be me." I tried my hardest to egg him on.

"Did his lady dump him?" TJ asked assuming this was the man's problem.

"No our government is screwing him," I replied, hoping for some sort of smart remark.

"Speaking of dishonest governments, do you recall being showered with insecticide by a low flying plane our first evening in Cuba? Remember how the bellboy kept reassuring our safety mentioning the government approved it. He went on to tell us his government would never do anything to harm people," TJ reminisced, grabbing a glass of juice.

"Remember while the Cuban was speaking, a huge black X appeared above his head."

The following day many people, including us, fell ill along the resort strip. The pesticide used was systemic and harmful to the nervous system. Unaware tourists blamed it on the food and water. Travelers need to pay more attention to airborne contaminants.

"People naively believe what they are told by government officials and big businesses," mentioned TJ effortlessly emptying his glass. "Remember when I was hired by that dental equipment repair service? The owner was eager at the interview. He hired me on the spot and put me straight to work. I spent the morning assisting a colleague with moving heavy broken sterilizers. My supervisor treated me to lunch. The moment I bit into my burger he asked me if I'd been vaccinated against Hepatitis and HIV. I was sick with horror and started shaking with anxiety, after working barehanded all morning. Thankfully I scrubbed down every time he did. I quickly dismissed myself from the table and rushed to call you."

"I remembered being concerned about you around bio-hazards the day before. Instead of paying attention to my intuition, I chose not to worry."

"I would have probably treated your concern the same way. Your insight might have caused me to look deeper into things before taking the job." TJ aired his feelings.

"Talking about diseases and dishonesty brings back an unnerving subject. I heard an interesting tidbit a couple of years ago from an acquaintance, who was a nurse. She was attending a meeting regarding pandemics. The woman was very concerned after hearing the main speaker say that SARS was going to be huge, but not as huge as H1N1. Back then, from what she knew H1N1 didn't exist, but the Swine Flu certainly did. The arrival of HINI frightened her, because of what she previously had heard during that meeting. She felt uneasy about the vaccine. Her biggest fear was the government was trying to eliminate some of the population. Out of fear, she refused to look deeper or to become immunized.

Governments and big business have become corrupt. Our only hope is in voting in good politicians who are untainted, but this is going to take time. Unfortunately we can't run without rules. Society isn't advanced enough to function that way. The dishonesty that presently reigns needs to be stopped. We need to be aware of what's going on around us. This is where spiritual openness instead of religion can play a big role in our daily world.

Chapter 6

Blinded by Faith

The dead are speaking and warning loved ones about their faiths. "Had I known then what I know now, I wouldn't have spent so much time on religion." This was from a deceased devout Catholic mother to her surviving daughter. "My religion misled me," a deceased Pentecostal Minister said to his living son.

Traditional faiths controlled their flocks through the fear of eternal punishment. This threat kept the worshippers in line and the religions in business. Many people perceived spirituality as evil. Millions are brainwashed. Blinded by faith, they fail to see the bigger picture. They jump to conclusions, passing judgment, which causes further damage instead of peace.

On a cold winter's day in downtown Edmonton, a Religious convention was breaking for lunch. Across the way I could see hundreds of people swarming the doors as they exited the facility. They rushed into the adjacent mall grasping the main doors seeking shelter from the bone chilling winds. These people fended for themselves only. Acts of shoving and pushing could be seen from the distance. Some even failed to notice others behind them, allowing the heavy glass doors to slam in their faces. A young man rushed to open the door for an elderly woman. After she passed through, he prompted her for recognition.

"Do I hear a thank you?" he hollered in agitation. The aggressor leapt in front of the woman trying to engage in eye contact. Caught off balance, she toppled helplessly to the floor.

Several people filed by without showing concern. Two elderly gentlemen stopped and helped the lady to her feet.

A nicely dressed woman from the scene waltzed up to my table. The dame swiftly grabbed a book and curiously glanced at the back cover. Disgust overrode her pleasant demeanor.

"Are you the author of this nasty book?" she inquired, as her body language declared war.

"Yes," I responded, stepping backwards to avoid the array of spit fleeing from her fiery mouth.

"You're of the Devil." She erratically hoisted her index finger, shaking the erect appendage in a scolding manner.

"There is the Pope, God and you! How dare you rewrite the Holy Bible."

"Lady, I didn't," I debated with her, lowering my tone. "This book is my life biography, not the Bible."

The raging lady lunged, positioning herself in my face. Her crimson face almost matched her red Christmas outfit.

"I'm a Christian. This is not of God," the crazed woman shrieked, her voice continuing to rise several octaves. In anger she thrust the book towards the crowd that was starting to gather.

The hand of a male bystander intercepted the projectile mid-flight. A piercing slap penetrated the air as the spine contacted his palm. "Yes," a victorious man's voice cheered, while contentedly eyeing the object in his hand.

"Lady," said the angry woman, "you'll never see the gates of Heaven. God will throw you to the depths of Hell!"

"I've already seen the gates of Heaven." I met her glare with a smile. In a huff the smoldering 'Christian' shoved her way into the crowd and disappeared.

"Excuse me," the athletic man who caught the book addressed me. He stood firmly cradling the book in his hands.

"Why did Jesus die on the cross?"

"The people crucified him," I responded, calmly meeting his glaring eyes.

"Wrong! Wrong! You're wrong, he died for our sins!" He roared like a lion. Threads of saliva could be seen perfectly strung from his top to bottom front teeth. The jugular veins on his neck popped to the surface with great intensity.

A middle aged woman stepped up and took her place beside him. "Obviously, you're not a Christian," she abruptly spoke as she flung her sliding purse strap back up her meaty shoulder. "Unless you're born again you will never experience the Kingdom of Heaven."

By then a full crowd was gathered.

A ginger-haired uniformed soldier stepped forward. "That's not true. I'm Catholic and we go to Heaven after the end of time," he strongly stated, straightening his posture. A woman could be hearing clearing a frog from her throat. "I'm a Jehovah's Witness and you are all wrong. Only Witnesses inherit the Heavenly Kingdom."

An attractive cowboy decked out in western attire rushed up to the lady almost putting her off balance.

"Your faith has brainwashed you. I used to be a Jehovah's Witness, until I watched my brother die, because he refused a life saving blood transfusion," he burst out while grabbing a book. "Plus, my aunt is Lutheran and had a near death experience last month. She went to Heaven and was met by her late husband. My aunt was told it wasn't her time yet and a force immediately delivered her back to her body. My uncle was a Lutheran his whole life and made it to Heaven."

An Asian woman standing patiently amongst the upheaval politely interrupted the group.

"I'm Buddhist and I will have an afterlife." She took great pride speaking up for her beliefs.

"No way, you worship false gods and idols. I don't want to hear from anyone crazy enough to worship pottybelly Buddhas," the mouthy soldier protested.

"At least you weirdo's are peaceful, unlike her." He arrogantly pointed in the direction of a young woman wearing a hijab. "The Muslims kill innocent people for a promised rewarding afterlife."

The poor lady looked mortified. This woman had a heart of gold and the aura to prove it. She quietly backed out of the explosive crowd and left.

"People, we all have souls; my book shares my authentic spiritual biography. I'm not here to preach or judge. I'm here to share my life story," I started.

"Excuse me, Miss!" interrupted a woman from the gathering decked out in purple.

"I'm a United Church minister. God is love. Spirituality is real. This author has a gift." This minister rushed to the table grabbing the book closest to the edge almost compromising the display. She whipped through the book like a pro, quickly skimming and scrutinizing the pages. Bystanders stood speechless, anxiously awaiting her opinion.

"My church needs to see this book. God's people need to understand spirituality of the soul in plain simple English."

"You should be ashamed of yourself, Preacher." hollered a rough leathery voice from the crowd as the crown of a fedora could be seen bobbing behind the front of the line.

"I'm an ordained Baptist minister. This is not of God." A grotesquely pock-marked face finally emerged from the thick crowd. This poker-faced Baptist continued to question her in a harassing manner.

"Where is the author's authority? Who does she serve?"

"Sir, where is your authority?" she snapped, inviting his challenge.

"God," he announced at the top of his lungs. He obnoxiously rolled his eyes while tilting his head toward the beyond.

"Your approach to ministry is egotistical," she retaliated in utter disgust.

"Has the Holy Spirit instructed you to behave in a judgmental self-righteous manner? I pray the Lord open your eyes and release you from these outrageous fears caused by man's interpretation of the Holy Bible in order to control the masses."

"This is why they should never let woman be preachers. You can't see the light ... you need to understand the passages ... and be strong enough to follow," he rebounded in a condescending air before strutting off into an adjacent store. The United pastor took her place back in the crowd and bowed her head.

"God, forgive him," a nun wearing a crucifix pendant on her necklace audibly whispered.

In the corner a Muslim family could be seen placing woven mats on the floor. The foursome peacefully started their worship ritual.

A man and his young son got down on their hands and knees on the gently placed rugs. The mother and daughter followed behind them in the same manner on their floor pads. Snickering could be heard coming from the crowd. While they were worshipping, mall security showed up and ushered an elderly homeless man out of the crowd.

"Come with us. You're not welcome," one of the guards scolded, while forcefully grabbing his arm.

The guard quietly scanned the crowd while removing the poor old soul back to the street. Minutes later the duo returned, making their way towards a Sikh dressed in a white robe and a black turban. Seconds later, the officers had him facing the pillar behind the group in a spread eagle position. The twosome hiked up his robe publicly revealing his thighs while searching him. After coming up empty-handed, the two idiots set him free.

Two young girls in the audience openly dangled silver pentacles from their necks, conveying covenant practices.

"Laura you're a medium. Do you dabble with magic?" one of the girls curiously asked.

"No, I'm not Wiccan," I replied. Tense agitation stirred through the crowd.

"Those two witches should be burnt at the stake," An elderly obese lady with a German accent shouted.

"Senile Nazi," one of the gals blasted her.

The heavy mammoth romped her way out through the enormous crowd. Three native girls snickered at the sideline, one could be overheard stating,

"Of all the faiths, our native beliefs make the most sense."

"Excuse me, Miss," I interrupted, taking a giant step towards the tanned girl.

"Why do you say that about your beliefs?"

Being caught off guard caused this young gal to blush and pause for a moment.

"In our culture," she started, "nature, animals, elders and the earth are respected. We probably have the most heightened spiritual experiences."

"Yeah, smoke another peace pipe, you useless squaw," an insensitive redneck roared from the back of the group.

"People, enough of these crude remarks! I came here today to show you my book 'Journey into Spirituality.' I am a psychic medium and this is my story."

"Do you talk to the dead?" a young lady with a pierced lip piped up.

"Yes," I answered, while pointing my finger towards my book. "This book has many details with loved ones and spirit guides communicating."

"Oh, awesome," she replied trying to maintain her composure.

"I'd like to welcome you all to my Connections Presentation, where loved ones come through and pass along messages," I addressed my captivated fans.

"This group is small enough that everyone can have a turn to ask a question or to receive a message from a loved one who's passed on. I will come to you one by one."

A few news reporters with cameras showed up on the scene. I made a mental note to stand straight and to smile. Being on camera is something I lack confidence in, but from what I hear I'm a natural. I needed to go ahead and do my thing.

"Excuse me, Laura," interrupted a news anchor with a television camera resting on his shoulder.

"I'm Nester Granger from NBB News Team. Is it okay if I tape this presentation for tonight's supper news segment?"

"Be my guest," I replied, grounding myself to work with my audience.

A lady's hand waved fiercely from a distance. "Oh please, I have a quick question."

I pointed towards her to answer her question. "Go ahead," I instructed the desperate lady.

"My husband is ill," she started, before sobbing uncontrollably.

I closed my eyes and went to Spirit. I was shown a black thyroid with the letter C beside it. The image went from dark to light green. Flashes of surgery and pills were revealed.

"I've been shown your husband has thyroid cancer. He's going to have surgery and take medication for the rest of his life. He's going to be okay." I looked directly at her, making sure she had absorbed what I said.

An impatient ghost of a deceased teenaged boy stood at his mother's side with a noose around his neck. I walked over and stood directly in front of the woman.

"May I come to you?" I spoke gently to the stranger in the crowd.

"Yes, do you have a message for me?" the quiet-spoken woman replied.

"Your son is here to see you." I watched the mom's jaw drop open in shock.

"He's sorry about leaving you stranded. Hanging himself was a selfish thing to do. He didn't realize how much his family loved him, until it was too late. He wants you to tell his father that he's very sorry and that he loves him."

"That's my Bernie," the distraught mother started to cry. "He wants you to say hello to Karen for him."

"Oh my God. Karen was his girlfriend." The stranger's eyes almost popped out of his head.

"Is he okay? Is he always around me? Did he see his grandfather yet?"

The letters "Y" "Y" "N" were drawn midair in smoke style above the mother's head. Decoded, these letters meant yes, yes and no. "Yes, he is okay and he's always around you. He hasn't seen his grandfather yet, because he's been earthbound. He's come to say good-bye." The ghastly boy quickly morphed into a light blue orb and pecked his mother on the right side of her cheek.

"Bernie kissed you. Did you feel a flash of warm pressure on your right cheekbone?"

The overwhelmed teary mother started to weep. "Oh my God, I felt that. Tell him I love him."

"He can hear you speak. Talk to Bernard like you used to." I calmly encouraged her.

"He's getting ready to leave us. He's going to check out the other side." A beacon of light flashed and Bernard was gone.

A woman's voice shot out from behind the front row. "Is there anyone around me?"

"Yes, approximately 50 people waiting their turn." Laughter erupted from the dense crowd.

"Your mother is standing behind you shaking her head in disapproval. You've never waited and you still don't." I watch the lady's face flush in embarrassment.

"I really needed to talk to her." My energy shifted once her mother connected. She started sharing images before her distraught daughter could go any further.

The name Stacy came to me, while an image of a black hand dipped into a jewellery box.

"Stacy has stolen your mother's jewellery." Paleness invaded the young lady's face. I was shown an image of a cash register at a store with a clear display counter with other valuable old jewellery.

"She sold ten valuable pieces of your mother's jewellery to a local pawn shop."

"We've been suspecting her. She's my sister-in-law." A look of anguish intercepted the daughter's face.

"My mother's ashes are missing and Stacy had them last."

An image of an urn being opened over a toilet bowl invaded my line of vision. This was followed by another sight of the same urn being thrown in a dumpster. A sudden wave of nausea hit me after witnessing the sickening cruel presentation. Is this something that I should publicly share? I pondered while staying in the moment.

"What I have to share isn't good. Can I have you see me later? This situation needs to be disclosed in private. I'll see you after the presentation."

I stopped beside a young lady. "May I share with you?" After receiving permission, I carried on.

"Congratulations on your pregnancy." Astonishment and joy embraced the pregnant mother's face. You had a fertility treatment days ago and a triple conception has occurred."

Bright energy from her aura beamed conception.

"I can't believe this is true. We've been trying for years and just had our first treatment two days ago. Three eggs were implanted. Does this mean I'm having triplets?"

"Yes, healthy triplets for you." Exposing her circumstances sent a wave of validating chills through my body.

A native lady raised her hand next.

"Go ahead," I pointed in her direction. An apparition of a young troubled lady stood to her right.

"My cousin recently died a horrific death. I need to know if she's okay."

"I'm being shown medical staff ignoring her. Then I'm seeing something about an ambulance bay. Your cousin is still earthbound due to the nature of circumstances surrounding her death."

The lady's face displayed shock. "My cousin walked into an inner city emergency room intoxicated looking for medical assistance. Triage staff turned her away. She stepped out into the adjoining ambulance bay and collapsed to her death. Can I get you to sign one of your books for me?"

"Sure," an indigo blue orb was floating around the table top close to where I was signing. I thought this was odd.

The lady returned in a rush back to my table. "There's something wrong with the front cover. The entire front cover is scratched. Can I please have a different one?" the shocked woman begged. I signed an undisturbed book and handed it to her.

I inspected the questionable book cover. At a distance the cover looked horribly scratched, but a closer look revealed an etched portrait of a woman. When I signed her book an orb hovered slightly above my hand. I remember gently pushing the entity away. This was a drawing from her recently deceased aunt.

A dying man with grey in his aura approached me. "Do you see my parents around me?"

"No, I don't see them around."

"I wanted to tell my mom and dad that I'm sorry for the pain and grief I caused them. I was addicted to heroin. I used to shoot up. I used to steal from them and others to support my habit," the man started to sob uncontrollably.

"I'm a recovered addict. I haven't touched anything in five years. I just found out that I'm dying from Hepatitis C. My liver is completely shot. I'm scared there is no place for me in Heaven." The man shook and sobbed intensely before pulling himself together.

"If you can get a hold of my parents, tell them I'm sorry and that I love them."

"Your parents can hear you. They see your actions. You need to forgive yourself. Heaven awaits you, for there is no Hell."

Spirituality of the soul and religion seem to be similar, but in reality they are very different. Spirituality pertains to the soul and its connection to the high power. Religion is big business, which is based on beliefs.

Chapter 7

Emergency

Emergency operators man the 911 switchboards 24 hours a day. We assume they are available to assist us.

An urgent call rouses a small town operator from a deep sleep. She dispatches an ambulance to a burning house instead of a fire truck. An egotistical police dispatcher circulates a woman's desperate plea for help to the complaints line; while her violent ex-husband is chasing her through a busy freeway.

Martha, a 911 operator, showed up unannounced at my door and rang the bell. Before I could answer the door, she had already let herself in.

"Laura, I really need to talk to you. I hope I'm not intruding." She started peeling off her jacket before I could say a word.

"You seem panicked. What can I do for you?"

"Last night ended up being a total disaster at work," she said, helping herself to one of my kitchen chairs.

I was shown Martha fast asleep at the emergency switchboard with nobody else in the room. Her head rested on top of her folded arms with answering gear firmly attached. "Oh Martha," I admonished, "you girls shouldn't be sleeping at work."

"But our boss lets us as long as we answer the calls."

I received a display of an ambulance arriving at a house fire. "A house burned to the ground," I said with alarm. "You dispatched an ambulance instead of a fire engine."

"How did you know that? Did the others tell you what happened? Or did you see it on the news and put two and two together?" She sat there completely flabbergasted.

"I didn't have to. Your guide showed me."

"It wasn't my fault my co-worker slipped out to have a smoke with her guy and left me alone. I didn't even know she was gone."

"Martha, that's not the point. You're handling life and death situations. Sleeping shouldn't be a part of this. Remember last week you were woken by a frantic mother with a choking toddler."

"That was terrible. I didn't know what to do. I started to panic and kept saying 'Holy Shit, do something.' My boss quickly took the call from me and started helping the desperate caller."

"You were sleeping and got caught off guard." "But you're not listening to me."

"I heard you fine. Had you been awake, you would have been able to cope. Martha, you're not being responsible.

"Laura, I'm scared they're going to fire me."

"I think you should give notice and find a different job, where moments don't count."

"You don't understand. We're allowed to sleep at work. We get paid major amounts of money to work the graveyard shift."

"You're missing the point here."

"What about my job?"

"What about their lives?"

"I need to know that I'm secure."

I connected with Martha's spirit guide again who was shaking her head no. She gestured me to lead Martha to the door. This was a new one for me. I gladly obliged her guide and showed her the way out.

"Martha, please leave. I'm not going to listen to any more of this"

"This isn't fair. You didn't answer me."

"Think on it, Martha. Search your soul. Perhaps you'll see the light," I commented, gently closing the door behind her.

I knew there were big problems in our district. In a small town of 60,000 people, the budget had had extensive cuts. During the night only two operators man the emergency switchboard. Four officers patrol the 60-kilometre area between 11 pm and 7 am. Ambulance services are not always available for the people living just outside the town.

Later that afternoon, I received a call from an elderly friend. "Hi Laura, do you have a few minutes?"

"What's up?"

"I was home alone resting after my chemo yesterday, when my nose started to bleed profusely to the point I was choking on blood as it flowed down my throat. I felt like I was drowning. In a panic I called my neighbor. She rushed over and immediately called 911. They told her to take me to the hospital. They felt it wasn't a serious emergency. The operator mentioned an ambulance would be at least a two hour wait."

"You sure deserve better treatment than that."

"I can't imagine what would have happened had it been a heart attack instead."

My other line started to ring. My friend heard it and quickly freed herself from my line.

"Hi, did I reach the psychic?"

"Yes, this is Laura speaking."

"I need to talk to someone." The caller was stressed and needed to be heard. "Can I come see you right away?"

Within the hour the ragged young woman came trampling through the door. Tears started to trickle before she was able to speak.

"I watched a young boy die yesterday. I just feel so sick. I can't stand it." She sat at the table and bawled inconsolably to the point her tears literally landed on the table-top. I offered her a tissue, but she chose to use her sleeve instead.

"He went right through me." Now she was wailing out of control and dry heaving at times. She was hard to follow.

In order to help her I needed to see. I connected with her guide for immediate assistance. I was shown her performing CPR on a lifeless boy. He'd been thrown from a red vehicle. At the moment of death his soul physically passed through her body. I was shown a preacher, his hysterical mother and a helicopter. Finally an apparition of the boy appeared. He was approximately seven, vibrant and smiling as if nothing bad had ever happened.

"You stopped to help the people at the scene of a horrific highway accident. A young blonde boy was thrown from the windshield of a red vehicle. He wasn't breathing and you performed mouth to mouth respiration."

The young woman burst into another crying jag. I let her be until she started to calm down. I reached out to hold her hands, which she allowed. I was able to have physical contact, which is important in keeping someone with you. I was going to need her stable for the remainder of the session.

"The boy's soul went through your body when he died. This really frightened you." She was almost back to square one, but not as bad. "What happened," I continued, "is very normal and nothing to be scared of."

"He went into my mouth and through my body. I don't know if he ever made it out." I released her hands as she started to wretch, obviously needing space.

"I'm so scared I don't want him in me. I don't want him in me." She became hysterical before eventually regaining composure. "The other people stood there uselessly watching. When I got up, there was a priest at the edge of the road on his knees praying. Why weren't these people helping? A medic vac helicopter showed up. I overheard one of the medics say. 'He's a goner make it look good.' Why would they cover up the boy's death by acting this way?"

"They did this for good publicity like the rest of society does."

"I need you to tell me the truth. Is the boy stuck inside my body? I dreamt of him last night."

"No the boy isn't stuck inside your body. You felt him leave the world. His soul went right through you. The soul can penetrate anything."

"Are you sure?"

"Yes, he's here with us right now."

"Is he upset with me for not saving him?"

"No, he's actually quite happy. He wants to thank you."

She started to cry again and the little guy skipped happily into the light chasing a moving beam of light.

Many people attend jobs on a dysfunctional level in today's tainted society. Their attitudes and general lack of responsibility is quite appalling. Diversity and harsh challenges that manifest will bring about some very crucial lessons. People will be experiencing unusual spiritual events which bring about a new awareness, such as this young boy in the story that went through the lady's body.

Chapter 8

Dire Consequences

The medical systems have become political and greedy. Unethical directors dictate medical activities within the hospitals. Administrators are disabled and unwilling to assist the public. Doctors remain quiet to protect themselves from repercussions.

Housekeeping staff could be heard screaming hysterically and hollering for help. Echoes of running feet frantically pounded the third floor hallway of this inner city hospital. Two frantic Hispanic girls ran to the nearest nursing station.

"There's a dead doctor in Day Surgery room 320," the horrified gal conveyed in a shaky winded voice.

Medical staff from the unit rushed to the scene.

"Oh my God, it's Dr. Drew," one of the nurses shrieked.

The prominent doctor's stiff corpse was lying face up between two vacant beds. A small pool of blood surrounded his head. An empty syringe remained protruding from his neck. The head nurse squatted beside his lifeless body, searching for a pulse.

"He's gone." She scrambled back to her feet. He's ice cold." "Press the help button," she demanded, yanking a sheet from the nearest bed and covering his corpse.

The speaker came on. "Hello, how can I assist you?" piped a crackling voice from the intercom.

"Staff emergency, room 320. One of our doctors is down. We need assistance."

Pounding soles and rushing bodies of the emergency team invaded the third floor hallway. Wheels of the crash cart squealed aggressively towards the scene. The responders ran into the room. Two men headed directly to the covered body and pulled back the sheet.

"Would someone call administration? We need a head doctor and a hospital official here. Someone call the morgue. Page security and have them secure the area," the lead team member rattled off in a calm controlling manner.

The hospital director and the head emergency room doctor showed up simultaneously.

"What's going on?" they demanded in unison, as if they were one.

"Dr. Drew is dead," the head nurse broadcasted, trying to keep her composure. A strong gut feeling overtook her.

Something was amiss. She was having difficulty comprehending the sensation. This was highly unusual for her to be caught off guard.

Two of Drew's colleagues showed up together seconds before the hospital coroner.

"What's going on?" one of the colleagues interrupted.

"Dr. Drew has been found dead," a nurse from the emergency team informed the doctors.

The two associates hovered over the dead doctor, taking control of the situation. The coroner stood next to them.

An associate broke the silence: "I knew he was depressed, but I didn't realize he was suicidal – see the needle is lodged perfectly into his jugular vein. He had just enough time to inject a toxic substance before dropping dead. Definitely self-inflicted."

"His death is a suicide," the Coroner ruled in an authoritative manner. "I need to run a toxicology report, to find out the drug he used. Let's pack him up and move him to the morgue."

"I'll call his wife," the associate's voice interrupted as he rushed out of the room.

Hours went by and the head nurse remained deeply disturbed. She kept sensing the presence of the late Dr. Drew. She repeatedly felt chilling sensations from head to toe. Goosebumps erupted all over her forearms, raising her delicate arm hairs. Entering the hallway she kept seeing dark shadows. Trying to sort things out, the charge nurse grabbed the master key ring from her drawer. Without a word to anyone, she snuck off on a mission.

She arrived at Dr. Drew's office and wrestled with the key lock for a moment, before popping open the lock. Becky sensed a rush of energy the second she stepped into his office. His office looked inviting as it always did, but now it felt empty. His portrait on his desktop caught her eye. Bursting into tears she picked up the framed photo of her late flame, Dr. Ernest Drew. Strong doubt took hold of her about his death being a suicide. How could a man she was so in love with kill himself? He recently planned a weekend getaway in Vegas for both of them. This so-called conference was nothing more than a cover for their romantic interlude. Her gut told her that happy content people don't commit suicide.

Taking a seat in his chair she leaned forward cradling her head in her arms. "Why is my Ernie dead?" she whispered in a barely audible voice, fighting back the onslaught of fresh tears. The sensation of a hand rubbing her upper back set her off.

"Ernie is that you? Give me a sign," Becky demanded as the lights flickered aggressively. "Are you okay?" The lights went out for a moment then came back on. A white feather appeared on the desk top. Beside it, a heart was etched into the thin layer of dust spread on the desk's surface. The word "help" was encased by the heart. Why was "help" displayed inside the heart? This evidence alone was disheartening. Becky retrieved the cell phone from her pocket and snapped a shot of the message.

Opening his desk drawer, she grabbed the phone book and flipped to the psychic page. After skimming the section for a few minutes the name Laura Laforce stood out. Nothing is coincidental, she surmised in her sorrow. She recalled hearing co-workers mentioning her name, claiming that she is an exceptionally gifted medium. This reference alone was going to have to be good enough for her. She picked up the phone and made an appointment for the same evening.

I sat across from my client preparing to read her. "Becky put your palms on top of mine," I instructed the distraught lady. The moment we joined hands, I closed my eyes and the visions started to come forward. Her deceased lover partially materialized beside her in a doctor's jacket, claiming he was murdered.

"Your sweetheart is here and he's been murdered. He says he loves you. His name starts with the letter E. He's a married man, leaving behind a wife and mistress. He was murdered at work by two doctors with the initials B and C. This murder was pre-meditated. The hospital director with the initial B is behind this." An image of a raspberry flashed before me, followed by a strawberry. "Berry," I blurted like a charade player claiming an answer.

"These unethical doctors were illegally harvesting and retailing organs to the black market. Dr. Drew recently started working excessively long hours. Having seniority, he was allowed longer operating room privileges. This severely cut into their profits. Dr. Berry paid his colleagues to finish him off."

"Oh my God, I knew something was going on, but I didn't know what!" Becky gasped as she started breathing erratically.

"Dr. Drew was hard of hearing. These associates snuck up on him. The skilled surgeon had plenty of time to locate and penetrate his jugular vein. A lethal injection was shot into his neck. They left the syringe hanging as a suicide ploy. The other doctor lowered him to the floor by his waist. Allowing him to drop at the last moment caused his head to contact the floor resulting in a pool of blood stemming from his nose. Both men wore surgical gloves, and quickly disposed of the evidence in the hospital incinerator.

"An innocent coroner was coerced by the doctors into ruling his death a suicide. He was completely unaware of what took place." I lifted my head and opened my eyes

Streams of tears ran down her cheeks. "You're bang on, I knew his death wasn't a suicide, but I couldn't comprehend what happened to him. There was tension between the doctors, but there was no reason for murder. Where do I go from here?"

"You should let the authorities know, but don't expect much of them. The police want proof, which is going to be almost impossible to provide." Before I could say any more, a wave of sudden sharp stabbing pains hit me. In desperation I tried to conceal what was going on.

"Are you okay?" she inquired, looking straight at me with concern. "You look as though you have seen a ghost."

"I'm fine." I struggled to keep my composure.

My client didn't need to be dealing with my situation. In my head I wasn't going to succumb to this, at least not yet. She thanked me for the session and headed out the door.

I gradually made it over to my recliner to relax. Before I could meditate, my phone rang. Jeff the Medicine Man was on the phone.

"Hi Laura, I see that you're struggling with pain again. Spirit has shown me that you have too many plastics in your system. The angels want you to protect your colon and cleanse your blood by drinking dandelion tea. You must fulfill your contract before you can heal."

"I don't understand. Are you trying to tell me that I need to drink dandelion tea to fulfill my contract?" I questioned him, because all of this was way too bizarre. "Why does this keep happening to me?" I complained in total frustration.

"It's part of your contract," he informed me in a matter-of-fact-tone.

"There is a reason for all of this. Soon you will understand, but today you need to rest."

Almost fours years earlier, an old neighbor stated that in five years everything I've been through would make sense. I needed clarity now. Later wasn't going to cut it. I thanked Jeff for calling and hung up the phone.

Earlier that day, I had dropped by a friend's herbal practice in sheer desperation. I could hardly stand on my feet. I stood in agony with tears in my eyes. My friend Kevin realized I was in trouble. "Kevin, I need help. My body is shutting down." I kept myself stable by holding onto the front counter. "I feel like I'm dying." I knew deep down that something was seriously wrong and so did he. We both knew it would only be a matter of time before things worsened.

"I'll make a concoction to keep the inflammation down," Kevin offered. "Hopefully it will minimize the pain. If things get worse you'll need to head to a hospital. I don't understand what's wrong with you. I've never seen fungus in anyone's irises like yours. You're very sick. Something is being overlooked."

I winced. "I've been through the hospital route for the past several years. Every time I show up, I'm promptly admitted, diagnosed and drugged. What would be the point in going there again? I never get anything resolved. Besides, Christmas is coming and I want to be home."

By then I could hardly stand and my legs were shaking. I paid him for the products and left, barely mobile. In the back of my mind I was going home and buying time. My focal point became spending Christmas with my family, nothing else.

Painful abdominal spasms set in as soon as I hit the cold winter air outside. My teeth chattered and the rest of me shook. I opened the car door and lowered my aching body onto the hard frozen seat. I sat, silently pondering my horrible situation. Before heading home, I asked Spirit for enough strength to get me home safely.

I pulled into the driveway and made it to the door in a slumped state. It took every ounce of energy to drag myself to the couch. I reached out for the faux fur blanket folded on the arm of the sofa. It took a lot to wrap it around my tender body before lying down. Rays of sunbeams teased the floor in front of the sofa.

"Spirit, am I going to die?" I whispered. The letter "X" suddenly manifested in midair.

"I don't understand this answer. Dying should be yes or no and nothing else. You guys are almost as bad as the medical field. I need more of an answer. Look here. I'm serious and I need help,"

I helplessly begged, but what was the use? I wasn't getting anywhere. All I understood was a problem labeled "X" just like in algebra. Math was something I'd never mastered.

How on earth was I going to figure this out? My life was on the line. I didn't have time to decipher their stupid codes.

"Spirit, please tell me what is wrong with me. I don't understand." I started to feel agitated. I closed my eyes to connect with Spirit. My intestines lit up in a glowing fluorescent white. This meant there was nothing wrong with them. I was stumped. Intense pain and severe inflammation didn't match up with the information I was receiving.

Weeks earlier, I had ended up in an emergency room with buckling abdominal pain. Upon arrival, I was assessed as being under cardiac distress. This was surprising to me. Apparently infection or severe pain can bring on heart complications. Morphine was administered to control the gut-wrenching pain.

I remember lying drugged and attached to numerous leads and lines in the hospital. A young doctor dropped in to reassess my situation. The physician mentioned to me that my unknown condition could be fatal. He urged me to consider having my entire colon removed as a preventative measure. The moment he left I asked my guides if I should listen. The word "NO" was repeatedly spelled out several times in huge black letters.

Tonight I followed Jeff's advice and sipped dandelion tea throughout the evening. Before falling asleep I received a vision of me on an operating table. A nurse was holding a mask over my nose and mouth. My head was surrounded by a green flimsy cap. I could see my thin pale eyebrows. Surgical staff wearing scrubs stood around waiting for me to lose consciousness. Dark cold energy encompassed the surgeon's aura. Even though the doctor seemed familiar I couldn't place him. This didn't look good. I couldn't comprehend why they'd be operating on me.

Fortunately I was at home, even though I probably shouldn't have been. For the remainder of the night, I drifted in and out of sleep. Relentless waves of pain kept peaking. My loving husband lay awake beside me begging his guides and angels to help me. He was able to ease my pain for short intervals throughout the night.

In the early morning hours, I was shown my insides illuminated in white. The photo resembled an x-ray, but displayed only internal organs. Both the large and small colons were okay, the liver was fine, the gallbladder and spleen appeared normal, the heart was fine and so was the diaphragm. A huge black letter "X" floated between the spleen and the kidney. My bones were left entirely out of the scene.

My problem was based on finding "X." The word "ME" was printed under the scenario on the right hand side. Now I had an answer, but nothing concrete enough to discuss with a doctor.

Every day became a struggle. Odd things happened that didn't make sense. Pain went up my spine to the point that I could hardly move. I couldn't even get off the couch. Thankfully my cell phone was in my pocket.

I called TJ at work and he immediately left for home. I called Jeff the healer and he started to lift the pain over the phone, so that I could function.

"Try not to panic. Your angels are telling me that this is part of your contract. The worst is almost over. You will get through this. The doctors don't know what they're doing. The rest is for you to find out."

"One of us must be bloody crazy," I gasped trying to breathe. Nobody in their right mind would have signed up for this amount of pain. No heavenly angel or guide should have permitted such an agenda, I thought to myself. I vaguely remember being about seven years old, knowing I was going to be very sick for a while when I was bigger. Perhaps this made sense, but I definitely wasn't going to own this any time soon.

A few minutes later breathing became easier. I must have fallen asleep out of exhaustion. The next thing I remembered was TJ softly speaking to me while holding my hand.

"Let me take a look at you. You look like you've been through the mill." He gently lifted my neck and sat on the sofa, resting my head in his lap. "I sure wish I knew what was wrong with you. This time it's different, but I feel it's all connected. I don't understand why the doctors can't find what's causing this. Let me figure out where we need to go for help." TJ shut his eyes and hounded his guides for answers.

"I'm being shown that something needs to move. I don't understand what it is, but I'm shown the chiropractor can help ease the pain."

TJ picked up the phone and made an emergency appointment with the chiropractor. I was seen as soon as we arrived. The doctor tried to figure out what was going on. My symptoms were unusual. I hadn't hurt myself or slept wrong or lifted anything. Nothing was out of place, but my entire body exhibited severe pain. The idea of a gallbladder problem surfaced. Some of the symptoms matched, but the rest didn't. TJ stayed home the remainder of the afternoon, making sure I was okay. He made dinner for us and cleaned up, then came sit with me.

"I'm sorry this is happening. I wish I knew how to stop it."

I worried he'd lose interest in me if it went on any longer.

"Something is seriously wrong with you," he reassured me, "but I love you anyways. There must be someone out there who can help. We just need to find him." TJ sat beside me, rubbing my cold feet as I lay on the sofa.

"Yesterday I saw all my organs lit up in white. A letter "X" showed up close to my rib area."

"Why didn't you say something?"

"I've only seen my body twice this way before."

"Did you understand what you were shown?"

"I understood that my insides were okay."

"Tell me about the other times? I'll see what we can put together."

"The first time I saw a letter "X," it was on my foot."

"That's when you had two pieces of glass in your foot and the doctor wouldn't listen." TJ mused before carrying on. "He was shocked when you returned with the x-rays he ordered and pointed this out. Then he tried to dismiss this as scar tissue. He was confident that glass would have a different appearance and refused to listen to you."

I nodded agreement: "That's when I went home and tuned into my spirit guides. They gave me vivid instructions about what I needed to do. Following their lead I drew the nasty pieces of glass out of my foot with a steaming hot teabag. Seconds later I sat staring at two jagged beads of glass resting on top of the compress."

"What about the other vision?"

"I was shown a surgeon holding up an illuminated colon."

"Where did that fit in?"

"I had a biopsy done and everything was normal."

"Obviously "X" indicates something is wrong. It seems to relate to foreign objects."

We tried to make the best of a lousy evening. TJ snuggled beside me in bed before kissing me and turning off his light. Moments later, his voice interrupted the silence.

"Laura, are you okay? I just saw a vision of someone being rushed to the hospital."

"Geez, you're a copycat. I was shown the same thing. Right now I'm fine, let's get some sleep." Wanting to sleep, I tried to avoid the topic. I was sick and tired of being sick and tired.

"I'm here if you need me."

I awoke to the sound of my own piercing scream. Sharp pains shot through my abdomen. My whole body shook, making it hard to speak. "TJ, TJ, I need help."

"Come snuggle up against me."

"I can't." By now I was crying.

"What's going on?" TJ turned on his light.

"It's got my stomach," I cried in sheer agony.

"What has your stomach?" he questioned me calmly while trying to see if he could move me.

"I don't know."

TJ got me in the car and raced to the nearest emergency room. I was admitted immediately. I was a shaking crying mess. Both my arms were being restrained by emergency staff as they feverishly tried to access veins, which rolled and disappeared. TJ stayed with me the entire time. I could feel the grip of his firm hand on my leg.

"You're going to be okay, they're almost done," TJ kept reassuring me in his calming voice.

"Hang in there, sweetie. We're almost done," a nurse calmly spoke, while still working with my horrible veins.

"We're going to give you some morphine to help with the pain," another nurse's voice added in a soothing manner.

Once the team finished, TJ was able to get in closer. He leaned over the bars of the stretcher and kissed me on the cheek. "I love you. Try to get some rest. Hopefully someone will figure out what's going on."

Succumbing to the drugs in my system, I drifted off. I woke up to the sounds of a familiar voice introducing himself to my husband. Dr. Mohammed, the resident surgeon, was at my side and he wasn't competent. My family doctor was on his case for misdiagnosis, not once; but twice. I remembered my family physician, Dr. Weller, speaking abruptly on the phone with this surgeon demanding answers years ago.

"How are you doing, Laura?" Dr. Mohammed addressed me in a caring manner.

"Terrible."

By the time he finished pressing on my belly, I was in excruciating pain.

"Laura, is Dr. Mohammed good?" TJ asked.

I remember shaking my head instead of replying. I was beyond talking. I couldn't explain anything in this condition. I can't understand why some people feel they function better under the influence of drugs. My spirit guides would send the odd message. Out of frustration, I'd let it go.

"Laura, you really scared me. I've never seen you that bad. I was on the verge of calling an ambulance." TJ pulled the blankets up to my shoulders, making sure I was warm enough.

"Sorry."

"It's okay. This isn't your fault."

Laying there brought back memories of events that had happened in this hospital before I met TJ. This was the same cubicle the paramedics wheeled me into when I was so weak from internal bleeding that I couldn't lift my head off the pillow without almost passing out. This was about the time that my family doctor retired knowing something was causing these flare-ups, but he didn't know what. This was the place where a doctor told me to go home; there was nothing wrong and I was wasting taxpayers' dollars. Dr. Mohammed proved him wrong days later finding abscesses deep inside. This was the place my deceased aunt and my late friend Tony appeared together at my bedside.

Thirteen hours after we arrived, I was being sent home. There were prescriptions, but no answers. Time passed by and my condition was still peaking. I tried my best to ignore it, hoping it would disappear. I kept bothering my guides for answers, only to see an "X," which wasn't reassuring or helpful. I struggled to make it through Christmas and New Year's without going to the hospital.

TJ and I were out shopping for groceries when a crisis hit. We were at the checkout when something deep inside me released like an elastic band. I stood doubled over, trying to breathe, as pain rampaged through my gut.

"Hon, are you okay?" TJ asked, rubbing my back.

All I could do was shake my head. I could sense TJ begging the angels for help. I felt a familiar tingle shoot through my body. I could see tiny angels circling around. Before long, TJ had me seated in the car and rushed me to the hospital. I quietly shut my eyes desperately trying to connect with my guides.

"Light up if I should go to the hospital. Go dark if we should head home." Immediately a beam of light took up my whole line of vision.

"Will they find anything?"

"Yes" was literally written in midair in huge white letters. The emergency room was full, but due to my dire circumstances I was attended to immediately. The nurse brought us into what reminded me of a jail cell. It had a metal toilet close to the wall with a tiny enclosure around. This brought back memories of the jail cell I had spent two nights in as a teenager.

"Excuse me, this is a jail cell," I interrupted the nurse, as my pain started to build with the stress of it all.

"Yes, it is our treatment cell for prisoners. It's the only bed we have available. I promise we'll leave the door open, if that makes you feel better. There is a proper bathroom down the hall if you need one." She was being completely honest with me, which greatly helped matters.

The doctor came in right away. Within minutes, an IV was started and morphine was administered to help ease the pain. Tests were run and x-rays were ordered. TJ remained by my side supporting me.

In the x-ray department they started to proceed as they normally do. Suddenly, the technician came to me. "Are you wearing anything metal?" she questioned me. "Let me check your gown, perhaps there's something in it." She frantically searched the gown almost like it contained something suspicious.

"I need you to take the gown off. I'll wrap you in a sheet instead." Her serious tone matched her actions.

"I can't. I'm hooked up to everything." I felt terrified and beside myself. Something was really wrong. I started to feel queasy.

"Let me help you with that." The older woman gently started removing the gown. In no time flat she had me draped in a sheet. "You're scared."

"Very." It took everything I had to avoid falling apart.

"Why don't you lie on the table and try to relax. I need take more pictures." She got right back to work and started moving me around and shooting different angles. "I'll let you know when I'm done." She darted in and out of the room several times, with a look of concern on her face. I lay there terrified, not knowing what she found.

"What's wrong with me?" I started to cry.

"There's metal in your chest. Let's get you back to emergency, so they can deal with this. I'll help you get your gown back on."

I managed to thank her before I started to sob harder.

TJ met us in the hallway. Right away he put his arm around me. "They found something?"

I nodded my head up and down trying to keep my composure. "They found metal in my chest."

"Did you see it?" TJ tried not to quiz me.

"No they're not allowed to show me." I wiped my tears on my hand.

"I don't understand how I could have something like that inside me."

TJ leaned over and kissed me on the forehead. "You're going to be okay. We'll get through this."

A misty grey fog suddenly appeared in the room.

TJ broke the silence. "Laura, I feel a strong presence in here."

"Yes, it's the ghost of a young man."

"Do you know what he wants?"

"Why are you here?" I questioned the male ghost telepathically.

"The doctor treating you diagnosed me with the flu. He wouldn't listen to me. My appendix ended up bursting. I died because he made a mistake."

"TJ, this ghost died from a ruptured appendix, because the doctor who's treating me wouldn't listen."

"Oh my God, I'll have to watch him like a hawk," TJ said.

The doctor showed up in my room moments later.

"Your tests are good and your x-rays fine. I'm sending you home with a prescription for inflammation and something for pain. Have you ever had a bleeding stomach?"

"Yes."

"Then only take a few of these. Don't finish the bottle."

"Why are you prescribing pills I shouldn't have?"

"I'll leave it up to you to decide if you want to take it."

"Doctor, if my x-rays are fine, why are the technicians concerned about metal in my chest.

"Did you ever have gallbladder surgery?" The physician asked. He seemed to be grasping at straws.

"Excuse me, Doctor," TJ interrupted. "we want to see the x-rays right now."

The doctor shamefully bowed his head. "Come with me. I'll show you."

We arrived at the counter where x-rays were reviewed. My past x-rays were still lined up on the lit-up viewing board. These included 2007, 2008, 2009, 2010 and 2011. The half inch piece of metal looked like a small calibre bullet. Spirit was right about where "X" was located.

"Doctor, look at this," TJ started. "This has been at the point of all her attacks, which have been gradually moving upwards. What is this piece of metal?"

"It's a surgical clip from a tubal ligation. See, the other one is still on her fallopian tube. I've been a doctor for thirty years, but I've never seen anything like this before."

"What is the next step?" TJ asked.

"I'm not a surgeon. I'm an emergency room doctor. My job is to save lives. This isn't a heart attack or acute appendicitis. She can go home," the doctor suddenly became livid and stormed off down the hallway.

"Let's get you home and into bed – I'll call our doctor's office in the morning." TJ helped me into the car and drove home. In the morning he secured a couple of appointments. I reported the emergency room doctor to administration and it landed on deaf ears. I called the College of Physicians and Surgeons and was told to call back after this issue was resolved.

The first physician I saw wanted to run more tests. He wasn't convinced a half-inch foreign object behind the spleen would cause symptoms.

Dr. Mohammed refused to help. "That's not my hardware. Call the doctor who did the procedure if you want it out," he arrogantly stated, unable to look me in the eyes. "I feel this isn't what's causing your problem anyways. Lots of those float around in people's bodies. I believe you have diverticulitis and you should probably have half of your colon removed."

A good friend's physician tried to help me, even though she wasn't allowed to take on more patients. This terrific woman knew what I was up against. She placed several calls trying to find a willing surgeon. "Laura, this clip could perforate one of your organs; It could cost you your life. A lot of these doctors won't help you, because this is a freak incident stemming from a careless surgeon. You need to be seen by a different hospital emergency room. Hopefully someone will see beyond the politics and remove it before something happens."

TJ and I had a few more visits to a variety of emergency rooms. Doctors insisted something else was causing pain. They wanted to run expensive tests and do unnecessary procedures. They pushed painkillers and antibiotics and x-rays and more.

One smart-assed resident found out what I did for a living. In quotations at the bottom of his report he wrote: "Patient claims to be psychic and claims to see surgery being performed." He was called away and I added the rest. "Doctor needs to take his head out of his ass and join reality."

The doctor who placed the clip thirteen years earlier forced me to wait six weeks for an appointment. He knocked on the door and announced, "Here comes trouble," as he and a student walked into the examining room where my husband and I sat waiting. This practitioner mentioned every unrelated excuse possible for my symptoms. I was even told the clips are meant to live in the body. He suggested we meet in another week or two after he was able to review my case with a general surgeon. At the next appointment he complained about missing records. Finally I had had enough.

"I want this removed within a reasonable length of time."

"I'm gynecologist. I'm not allowed to operate up that high. I'd have to bring in a general surgeon to assist me."

"Bring a general surgeon in. I want both clips removed."

"Getting the one off the tube is easy and I'll get help with the other one if I need to."

Before he left the room he turned to me and said, "I'm not promising you anything." Something wasn't sitting right with his energy. I shut my eyes to connect with Spirit. "Is he lying to me about this other surgeon?" Everything lit up brightly. "Do I have other choices?" Everything went black. My guides kept showing me "2X" repeatedly.

"Are you okay?" he interrupted. "You shut your eyes and completely zoned out."

"I felt a little woozy, but I'm fine," I replied, hiding my ability. "Can you tell me the name of this other surgeon?"

"There are always general surgeons on standby. I'll call one in if I need help. That's the advantage of being in a big city hospital."

I knew he wasn't trustworthy years ago. I was sent to him to figure out why I had severe cramping and no cycles. He was the one who suggested the tubal to begin with. He first labeled me as having polycystic ovarian syndrome. A week after his diagnosis he called me to tell me about a fantastic new drug, which was curing this particular disorder. He told me to drop by his office and pick up the prescription. I heard on the evening news that night that this drug was being pulled because people were dying from liver failure after taking it. He wrote a prescription for a diabetic drug instead, which made me terribly ill. Next he changed his diagnosis to an allergy to the pill and offered the tubal ligation. I was leery, but dismissed it as fear and took him up on the offer.

A month later, I still had the problem as well as pain from the procedure. Another doctor found a blockage and surgically removed it, resolving the issue.

Now I had no choice but to deal with him first. The doctors are very political. If you mess something up, you fix it. If a hospital opens you up, no other hospitals will touch you.

Over the next several weeks, Spirit kept showing me different displays of operating rooms. They kept drawing out the number two and letting it fall sideways. Then I was shown two stripes lying across my stomach. I didn't understand what was being shown. I thought they were trying to humour me. Even if this was a warning, I didn't have a choice.

The surgical date finally arrived. I was wheeled to a waiting bay outside the operating room with TJ at my side.

"Laura, I'm tempted to join that doctor in the operating room. I don't trust him. If I'm watching he's more likely to get the job done."

"I don't trust him either, but I don't have any choices."

Two nurses dropped by and introduced themselves. Then the surgeon showed up and introduced two young female students that he was bringing in to assist him. TJ kissed me good-bye and wished me luck. Before I was wheeled into the suite, the surgeon resurfaced at my side.

"Remember, I'm not promising you anything."

My nerves were shattered. Tears kept streaming uncontrollably. Through the tears I could see my Spirit Guide bowing his head shaking it NO. The same nurse I'd seen in an earlier vision firmly held a gas mask over my nose and mouth. I struggled to pull away and lost consciousness while doing so.

TJ sat waiting in my room when this doctor approached him from a distance. "Laura is doing fine. Here's the clip from her fallopian tube. I couldn't find the other one. I can't help your wife."

They had a tough time waking me up. I don't remember seeing or hearing any staff afterwards. From what I heard,

I was brought up to the day ward unresponsive, and remained limp for hours. I remember hearing TJ's voice as I started to come around, but I couldn't see him. Eventually I had tunnel vision, where I could see through a spot the size of an orange and nothing else. I don't even remember being released from the hospital.

The following morning I saw one clip in a bottle on the bedroom nightstand. Something was wrong, but I didn't know what. I was in more pain, but at least I could see. I lifted my covers and looked at the covered incisions. Everything was done below the navel, but the loose clip was up past the ribs in the diaphragm. I was sure the one in the jar was retrieved from the fallopian tube. Swearing under my breath, I snuck out of bed while TJ slept.

I slowly made my way to our office to look up a surgeon. I lowered my aching body into my chair and started flipping through the telephone directory. Frustration set in when I realized I couldn't see clearly from yesterday's anaesthetic. I ended up using a magnifying glass to search the directory through the blur. It took a couple moments, but I eventually found a number and dialed.

"Good morning," an extremely tired woman's voice answered my call.

"Did I reach a surgeon's office?"

"Yes, but you're calling awfully early," she politely answered.

"I'm calling because I need help." TJ walked into the office looking very concerned and grabbed the phone. Within minutes I was back in bed beside him.

"The doctor didn't get the clip," I started to cry.

TJ gently rubbed my shoulder. "I know. I'm sorry that happened to you. I tried to tell you last night, but you were completely oblivious to the conversation. You had absolutely no reaction when I told you."

We spent weeks, which turned into months, trying to get the help I needed. I attended many appointments. My spirit guides showed me images of the office and the doctor involved. The doctors refused to help me. They'd blame the symptoms on other conditions such as IBS, diverticulitis, diverticulosis, Crohn's disease, rare bowel inflammation, irregular heart rhythms, digestive disorders, kidney stones, gallstones, colitis, celiac disease, hormonal issues, and the list went on. They'd tell me the clip could never cause damage or illness. They even mentioned the pharmaceutical companies deemed the clips safe. They'd try to talk me into other procedures, medicines and diets. Eventually I had heard enough. This was my body and I was in pain. I needed surgery and I wasn't insane.

Out of pure desperation, after exhausting all my available options, I turned to the politicians. I had nothing left to lose, except my life. I called the local representative in my area and told her my story. She took my name and number. Then she invited me to a health care forum to be held the same evening in an adjacent town. This discussion was going to be based on the looming health care crisis.

The moment TJ arrived home from work, I ran the whole idea by him. At first my husband refused to go.

"TJ, I understand how you're feeling, but I'm in the middle of a personal medical crisis. This one's based on our sub-standard healthcare system. Doctors and reporters are going to be there."

"And what's so great about that?"

"It's a chance for me to be heard. Maybe I can find the help I need." Even if TJ said no, attending this function meant the world to me.

"I guess I'll come with you. I don't want you out there alone in your condition."

"After supper I'm heading out make enlarged copies of my x-rays."

"Why?"

"I want to expose myself at the forum, so the world can see." A naughty smirk danced across my lips.

TJ sighed. "You sure don't take no for an answer."

"I'm not done living yet. I'm going to help myself. I have a chance to find a doctor or a reporter who is willing to help me. The public is going to be mortified when they see what has happened to me." I looked up to meet his gaze while awaiting his reply.

"Count me in. This ought to be interesting. Life isn't dull when you're on a mission."

We arrived and mingled with the crowd exposing my x-rays. I took a seat beside TJ, as the meeting was called to order.

"I'm Gary, your psychiatrist host for the evening," he rattled off in a light-hearted manner. "I'd like you guests to take a moment to introduce yourselves around the room."

"I'm Laura Laforce; I'll be the acting psychiatrist for the evening," I addressed the crowd, knowing the speaker wasn't a doctor. I couldn't resist inviting myself to compete for the position.

"Are you a psychiatrist?" he curiously questioned, looking shocked.

"No, I'm a psychic medium, but I could easily pass for a shrink."

"Do you see the dead?"

"Yes."

"Are there any around us right now?" he curiously quizzed, looking slightly apprehensive.

"Yes, there are some loved ones with us right now. Your mother is standing beside you. She died before you had a chance to say good-bye."

His jaw almost hit the floor.

"There is an angel in the corner behind the lady dressed in red." I pointed towards the woman across the room from me.

"Oh, I'd better stop while I'm ahead. This isn't what we're here for."

My enlightened introduction surprised several people. Afterwards, the others attending the meeting quickly introduced themselves, one by one, in an orderly manner around the circle before the meeting started.

A man walked up to me after the meeting ended. "I'm Dr. Davis, an emergency room doctor. That brief presentation was impressive. My father died last month and I've been missing him. Do you see him anywhere around me?"

"I saw your father standing beside you earlier and he looked great. He wanted you to know that he is proud of you."

"That's such a relief. I was hoping he was okay. Can I see those x-rays of yours?"

"Yes."

He reached over and grabbed the films and stood silently studying them. "I can't believe they're refusing to help you. This foreign body is dangerous and toxic to your system. I sure hope it doesn't perforate one of your major organs. Somebody needs to remove this. It's going to be hard to find a willing surgeon. These doctors want the easy jobs with lots of money and limited hours. Is it alright if I call around?

"Yes."

"Perhaps one of my colleagues with operating privileges might be willing to help you. Can I have your number?"

We exchanged numbers and I thanked him before heading for home. Several days later Dr. Davis called. He needed more time to deal with my situation. Other doctors were refusing to listen to him, but he wasn't about to give up.

Strong messages from beyond were being sent from my guides. These included interesting images, sounds, and words. I was shown a team of surgeons operating. A surgeon's arm was revealed holding a scalpel. A friendly nurse was smiling and comforting me. I heard the sound of metal landing on metal. This terrified me the most. I wondered if I'd wake up during surgery. I've come through conscious sedation three times in a single procedure in the past. Before falling asleep, I was looking at the top end of a stretcher accompanied by the sound of rustling paper. I was shown an oxygen panel at some point in the middle of the early morning hours. The following evening I was on the verge of falling asleep when a vision caused me to jump. "Holy Shit, that was close." I laid there trying to digest this latest show.

"What's going on?" TJ asked, making sure all was fine.

"A monochrome cube van marked with "A" "F" sped towards me and quickly turned, stopping along side me." I snuggled up to TJ trying to calm myself down.

"Sounds like an ambulance." TJ piped up.

"I didn't see any flashing lights."

"Remember you were caught off guard and saw this in black and white. You've been shown vehicles before," TJ confidently replied.

"Yes, in full color – none of them were moving like that."

"There's always a first time. Let's try to get some sleep, my dear. You need your rest – I love you." TJ passionately kissed me before turning off his light.

I gently held his hand hoping this would all be behind us soon. I wondered why I was being fed all this information, but not receiving the help I needed. A solid black heart suddenly took my line of vision; a curved arrow came out the bottom of it pointing downwards. This caused me distress. I hoped this wasn't my heart I'd seen in a vision, but perhaps something I was going to witness.

The following morning was a nightmare. I woke up feeling extremely ill. The phone rang several times. I could faintly hear TJ's voice from the kitchen speaking to the caller. I felt so awful that I allowed myself to drift back to sleep.

"Laura," TJ tried to wake me from my sleep.

"A Doctor Jones called me twice. He's waiting to see us in emergency."

"I don't want to wait in a busy waiting room. Just bring me something for the pain."

"You ate light last night. You haven't had breakfast or anything to drink. Maybe this doctor can arrange for emergency surgery."

"But it's Saturday and nothing like that is going to happen."

"When we get to admitting all he wants you to say is your belly really hurts and nothing else. He wants us to request him when we check in. He's going to examine you and take some x-rays before he can make a phone call."

To me this sounded easy; almost too good to be true.

"Let me grab your comfortable pants and a sweatshirt. I think this maybe worth our while," TJ insisted, while rummaging through the drawers to find comfortable clothing. "This pleasant doctor sounds like he knows what he's doing. He's going to be keeping an eye out for us at the front desk. He's says the emergency room is almost empty."

When we arrived at the hospital, I instantly recognized the doctor behind the admitting counter. He was shown to me in a vision weeks before. This was someone I could trust to get me the help I needed. I didn't acknowledge him nor did TJ. We didn't want to unfairly expose this dedicated man.

The nurse looked up from the admitting counter. "What brings you in here today?"

"My belly really hurts." I was in excruciating pain, but I desperately tried to contain it.

"Nurse, she looks awful. Let's get her into the examining room now," the doctor behind the desk ordered.

Dr. Jones started tending to me immediately.

"I heard through the grapevine that you were sick, but you're worse than I anticipated. I'm ordering some tests and we're going to take care of you."

"Thank you." TJ and I spoke at the exact same moment.

Emergency room staff came in and started all the necessary procedures I'd been through many times before.

Once the pain was under control, I was whisked off to the x-ray department. A few minutes later, TJ overheard Dr. Jones on the phone with a surgeon about my case.

Dr. Jones arrived back in the room minutes later.

"Laura I have good news. A surgeon by the name of Dr. Mohammed is willing to see you. I'm transferring you over to the General to be seen. Please don't drink or eat anything. I'm keeping your IV in and we'll give you more morphine before we send you off. Right now you're ready for surgery, but he gets to make the final call. All I want you to do is lie there and be the suffering patient. Laura, you're excellent at advocating yourself, but your husband needs to do all the talking. This doctor is an Arab; because you are a female, you're a second class citizen in his eyes. Do you understand?"

"Dr. Jones, that doctor won't help me."

"How do you know? Didn't you know you can talk anybody into doing anything?"

"I can't make people do anything. Everybody has choices. Dr. Mohammed recently refused to help me. He's made several misdiagnoses on me in the past."

"This time it's different. He's agreeing to see you. Your husband is going to do all the talking. He'll listen to him. You need to give this person another chance. Your life is at risk. This clip is toxic to your body. It's like a poison. This foreign body could potentially puncture your internal organs. I'm sending you back to the hospital that you went to when you first became ill. These hospitals are political. That was the facility which first started to treat you."

"Thank you, doctor." TJ reached out to shake his hand.

"TJ, remember you need to advocate for Laura. Make suggestions. Take this doctor aside, butter him up and appeal to him. In his Muslim eyes, Laura is your property."

"I'll do that, Dr. Jones."

I lay there feeling quite flustered with the idea of being a second-class citizen. Had my life not been on the line, I would have never agreed to this. I closed my eyes to connect with my guide. "I'm scared this doctor isn't going to help. Am I right?"

Bright fuchsia pink filled my line of vision and a thick black "O" was drawn on top. This verified what I already knew: Dr. Mohammed wasn't going to help.

Shortly after I settled into the other hospital, Dr. Mohammed showed up. He came in and re- introduced himself and started re-evaluating my situation.

TJ stood beside me talking to this doctor. "I'm glad you're able to see my wife on such short notice. I heard that you're an excellent surgeon. My wife deserves the best."

"She sure seems familiar, but I can't quite place her." Dr. Mohammed looked a little puzzled.

"I'm sure a fantastic surgeon like you has tons of patients, which would make it hard to recognize everybody."

"Your wife is in a lot of pain. She seems to be extremely sick. I'll have the nurses give her more morphine to keep the pain under control."

"Doctor, my wife has a loose clip behind her spleen. Would you consider removing it? Being the surgeon you are, this would probably be a relatively simple procedure. You could probably have it removed within the hour."

"I don't know what we're dealing with. I need to see her x-rays." He and TJ went across the room and started to review them.

"I'm not going to be able to operate. Surgery would be extremely dangerous."

"Leaving this in could kill her." TJ looked him directly in the eye.

"I don't know what the risks are, but I feel they outweigh leaving it in. Your wife could be far worse than she is right now. Surgery has risks. Her spleen could rupture. She could lose a kidney. She could hemorrhage to death on the operating table. There's a chance I could paralyze her, because this clip is close to the spine. I'm sorry, I won't do surgery, but I'll send her for a CT scan tomorrow."

The staff rushed in a young man into the next bed. He was complaining about not being able to breathe. Immediately I jumped to the conclusion that he must be the black heart that I had seen in an earlier vision. I really didn't want to be in the same room with him. I was concerned about feeling his pain on top of my own.

I was loaded with painkillers before they sent me home. TJ drove us home. Then he helped me into bed. I lay in bed trying to sort out the hectic day. I decided the black heart and the oxygen pertained to the guy in emergency. The rest really didn't matter. I lay awake stressing about the CT scan the following day at another hospital.

The next morning TJ drove me to the hospital where I was booked for a CT scan. I was loaded up with dye. I kept begging Spirit to be with me. I'm terrified of the dye. People have had deadly reactions from this dye. It's been known to have adverse reactions. I'd survived this twice before, but that didn't help matters. I have had life-threatening reactions to other drugs in the past. I felt terrified being alone inside a machine, facing the powerful rush of the contrast medium, which was injected through a machine into my veins. Everything burned and tingled throughout my body, as the dye raced through my system. I was a sobbing mess by the time the test was over.

TJ brought me home. After lunch he went to work and I went for a nap. Two clients interrupted me from my sleep. I had to let them go. I could hardly breathe. I tried to go back to sleep when one of them called back again. He was concerned and checking to see if I was okay. That's when I realized my chest was aching and my heart was pounding. I called the health advice line looking for reassurance. I hung up on the nurse when she suggested an ambulance should be called. I called TJ at work. He was extremely worried, because he had been feeling chest pains over the past half hour. TJ left for home and an ambulance was called.

A pleasant 911 operator stayed on the phone with me. Minutes later I heard the sound of blaring sirens. My chest hurt as my heart pounded out of control. I tried my best to remain calm. I shut my eyes. Through remote viewing, I watched the emergency vehicle racing towards me.

A few minutes later, two paramedics rushed through the door. They started to access my situation. I sat hunched forward trying to breathe. Oxygen was administered. Leads were placed to monitor my heart.

"Can you lean back and rest your head against the couch?" The pain was physically debilitating. I couldn't move. The paramedic grabbed a cushion. "Here, dear," he announced as he slowly ushered me into a better position.

TJ arrived home and raced through the door looking concerned. It was a relief to have him home. He sat across from me, staying out of the paramedics' way.

"Did she tell you she had a CT scan this morning?"

"No, she hasn't said much," one of the medics answered.

"Get my x-rays," was all I could manage. He returned seconds later and showed them to one of the paramedics.

"Oh, this doesn't look good. It's close to her aorta. This could be interfering with her heart." The previously calm paramedic struggled with what he'd seen.

"This could be enough to cause cardiac distress." His partner whipped her head around to catch a glimpse of what was going on.

"Oh my God, what is that?" she asked, caught off guard.

"A clip from a tubal ligation." TJ informed her.

"What the hell is that doing under her heart?"

"It broke off and travelled upwards."

The head medic quickly finished his assessment. "We're taking her to the city, where there are specialized doctors. She's in distress and needs proper help. We're going to take her out to the ambulance and start an IV and meds."

I was helped onto the stretcher and covered with two crinkling paper sheets. The decals on the side of the ambulance read "A" "F" Ambulance and Fire, identical to what I'd seen in an earlier premonition. As soon as they loaded me into the ambulance, TJ quickly sped off to the hospital. "Spirit, please help me get through this," I silently begged, fearing for my life.

An IV was started on the second attempt. Several doses of morphine were administered on the 70-mile trip into town. Aspirin was given to thin the blood in case this was a heart attack. Heart tests were repeatedly run.

"Laura, I need to ask you something," the concerned paramedic started.

"Has there been a problem with machines not picking up vital signs on your body before?"

"Yes."

"How do they handle things?"

"Manually."

"Thirty more minutes to arrival," the driver announced. "Are we cool?"

"Cool," my attendant replied. He sat beside me with my arm resting on his lap, keeping track of my weak pulse with his fingers on my wrist.

Within an instant I was more relaxed. I don't know if it was the morphine, his energy, or a combination of both. Periodically the driver would randomly announce minutes to arrival, making sure things were okay.

TJ was already waiting outside the ambulance doors when we arrived "Hang in there, love. You're going to be fine."

Due to shortages in the system, a bed wasn't available even though they'd radioed ahead. The paramedics pulled my stretcher in through the double sliding doors of the ambulance bay and continued treating me.

TJ's cell phone rang. Dr. Jones's nurse from the other hospital was on the phone. She had a sudden premonition of something being very wrong with me. From what I heard, she was mortified when she found out what had transpired. Minutes later, Dr. Jones was on TJ's cell phone pumping for information.

Moments after Dr. Jones got off the phone, I was wheeled into a room with an oxygen panel. This was identical to what I seen in a vision. A doctor came in to assess the situation and barked out several orders to his staff.

TJ slipped out with the attending doctor to review the results from my earlier CT scan at the desk across the way. The clip was floating in fluid right behind the spleen, above the kidney, half an inch from the small intestine, three inches from the aorta and right beside the diaphragm.

"It's okay for these to be floating around in the body," the physician attempted to persuade TJ.

"Your wife is overweight and has probably had a heart attack. Does she have heart trouble?"

"No."

An incoming call for the doctor interrupted their conversation. TJ returned to my side and told me all about what was found. Suddenly a small crowd of doctors gathered outside my cubicle. Their shadows could be seen through the curtains.

"A nosy Dr. Jones called my cardiac unit. He told me how to treat a patient by the name of Laura Laforce," his tone was livid. This official was furious.

"How dare he tell me give me orders. I'm his superior. I trained that bastard myself. How dare he run my show?"

The doctor assigned to me quickly whipped my curtain open and said, "Did you folks hear that?" I could see shadows of his peers on the other side of the drapes.

Black flashed before my eyes from Spirit indicating not to acknowledge. "No, Doctor, I didn't hear a thing, and my husband's hard of hearing."

TJ sat there looking clueless, following my lead. After the curtains were pulled closed, my loving husband winked at me. I felt uptight and upset. The boy's club was pissed off. I was very sick and depended on their care. I was hooked up to numerous monitors, tubes and oxygen. I was being bullied by the people who were supposed to be helping.

The moment TJ left to plug his parking meter, the disgruntled doctor noticed and suddenly paid me a visit.

"You've had a lot of x-rays and CT scans. I'm ordering another chest x-ray for you and an x-ray of your heart. You're well beyond your safety limit as far as x-ray regulations go. I'm sending for these tests, but I would advise you to be very careful. I'm going to run other tests to rule out whether or not this was a heart attack. You're going to be with us for at least another sixteen hours. We won't release you until we know what happened." He used intimidation as his tactic. "Your friend, Dr. Jones, has asked us to refer your file to a surgeon he's requested. After we're done assessing you, I'll entertain his absurd referral. He wants you to be assessed by this doctor, because he swears up and down that you need surgery. Personally I think he's full of..." His pager went off mid-sentence. He rushed out of the room to attend to whatever was going on.

An apparition of a woman surrounded by an orange aura appeared. She leaned over the rails and smiled directly at me. "Don't worry. You're going to be fine. You're luckier than the others in here." The beautiful angel from Heaven momentarily stood at my side, then disappeared..

TJ came back from plugging the parking meter. He gently cupped his warm hand around mine. "Did anything happen while I was gone?"

"The cardiologist who's pissed off with Dr. Jones paid me a visit. Then an angel dropped in and told me I was going to be okay, unlike the others."

"Sounds like a taste of Heaven and a glimpse of Hell," TJ added, attempting to lighten the tension.

A different cardiologist dropped in to chat with us. "I'd like you to do a stress test. If your runners were here, would you be willing to run on a treadmill?"

"No, I'm not willing to run with a piece of metal the size of a small calibre bullet resting under my heart."

"I could inject you with a dye instead that will speed up your heart, while our machines will pick up the images. Does that sound easier?"

"No, I'm not doing that either. I don't want anything else injected into me."

"Only a small percentage of the population has had an adverse reaction to this dye."

"Doctor, she's had life threatening allergic reactions to drugs. She's not doing this," TJ interrupted

"Do you exercise, Laura?"

"I used to, but not since I've been sick."

"You know you're going to get fat if you don't exercise."

"You think!?! I have bigger problems. I have a surgical clip floating in my chest causing medical problems. Don't you find that concerning?"

"Are you going to do the stress test or the dye test?"

Now he was leaning right over the bars looking me directly in the face. Shutting my eyes was the only way to block his repulsive presence.

"I'm talking to you and you're not answering me. That's a very rude thing to do."

"Excuse me, Doctor, she's had enough for today," TJ jumped in, protecting me.

"I really don't think you're capable of running on a treadmill for ten minutes when you're out of shape. I'm ordering that dye test for you. The hospital will call you tomorrow with a date and time." He rushed out of the cubicle after announcing his decision.

"Oh, Babe, I'm sorry that arrogant bastard treated you that way. You don't have to attend anything he books."

"Don't worry. I won't."

I was eventually released from the cardiac unit. A heart attack was ruled out without x-rays. All these specialists refused to acknowledge the clip was causing chaos. They insisted that major illnesses still needed to be ruled out. They wanted to do extensive costly testing, instead of dealing with the real problem.

I came home to a ringing phone. "Hi Laura, this is Connie from your family doctor's office. I'm calling you to tell you that he's heard enough about this clip. He doesn't want to see you any more. He says the other doctors don't believe you. He tells me to tell you that nobody wants to help you. Dr. Jones doesn't even really believe you."

It took every ounce of energy I had not to lose it with this back-stabbing bitch. "You've changed your tune. You were shocked when you saw my x-rays. You were the one who told me you'd find a surgeon to remove this. I feel you've been pushed into making this call. Correct me if I'm wrong." The phone went silent before I heard the click.

I closed my eyes and connected with my spirit guide.

"What's going on?" I was shown that the cardiac doctor from the hospital was behind this. I kept receiving vivid details about an upcoming visit with another surgeon. I could see the office and her face. I kept hearing different pieces of the conversation.

"I could make you far worse." The female's voice lacked confidence. "Those are meant to be in the human body."

"You're refusing to address an underlying major illness."

"If you don't start dealing with things, you could die."

By the time morning came I was fairly spent. I decided to attend this appointment even though I knew the outcome. It was extremely important that I keep jumping the hurdles as they were presented.

Upon entering the office everything was identical to what I'd been shown. The doctor's appearance and speech were a dead ringer of what I had heard the night before. I stood up in frustration, ready to walk out.

"If you don't start dealing with things, you could very well die," appallingly fell out of their mouths at the very same time. I grabbed the door handle and walked straight out of her office without saying another word.

I received an interesting call from my retired doctor's office manager.

"Hi, Laura. You have a referral that just arrived, for a surgeon's appointment at ten a.m. tomorrow. I don't understand why anything has been sent to us. As you know, Dr. Weller retired before Christmas. It's a good thing I was here packing up the remaining files." She gave me the address before hanging up.

"Who referred me?" I asked out of curiosity.

"I don't know. Things seem to be illegible. Don't worry about that. It doesn't really matter."

"Thanks for calling me. I really appreciate your kindness." I hung up the phone trying to piece together the rest of the puzzle. The following day, I arrived at the doctor's office a few minutes early and filled in the necessary forms.

I sat quietly in the examining room awaiting the arrival of the surgeon. He came into the room and extended his hand.

"I'm Dr. Kelly, and you must be Laura," he said in a very polite manner. I shook hands with the pleasant surgeon.

"I understand you've seen a lot of doctors lately."

"Several."

"I've read your reports. I understand a surgical clip has broken off from your fallopian tube and migrated through your body causing you grief. Can you show me where you're hurting?"

He examined the area near the spleen. "I'm willing to remove this, but it's going to be risky. Right now you're in a lot of pain. Your life will be at risk when I open you up. This could cost you your life. Do you understand?"

"Yes."

"This could cost you your spleen. Do you understand?"

"Yes."

"This could cost you your colon. Do you understand?"

"Yes."

"Are you prepared to cope with any of these issues?"

"Yes, I deal with what it already does to me every single day. Having surgery gives me the opportunity to get better. This clip has a sharp edge. It has the potential to puncture any of these organs at any moment."

"Yes, that's correct. Right now it's floating in fluid behind your spleen, but its path is unpredictable. It's traveled through your entire abdomen. Now it's in your chest. I need time to study your case. This surgery is very dangerous. I'm going to make four incisions and I'm going to use a fluoroscope to help locate the foreign object. I need to have you blood-typed. You may require a blood transfusion should something go wrong. I'm going to take all the precautions possible, including blood thinners, ahead of time. I'm going to handle this like spleen surgery. If your spleen ruptures you're not going to be able to fight off germs. I'll have you vaccinated before you leave the operating room if this happens. You'll be given antibiotics before surgery even starts. Please keep in mind your life will be on the line."

"Doctor Kelly, I understand the risk and I'm okay with it. I'm at risk either way."

"True, but I'd feel horrible if you died at my hands."

"Go ahead and operate. You're a fine surgeon and I'm going to be fine."

"Can I have the name of your family doctor, so that I can send him my report?"

I stood there speechless trying to figure out what to say. After that nasty phone call from the new family doctor's office, I was shocked. My old doctor's office was closing as of today, so that wouldn't work either. I still wasn't even sure who referred me to this surgeon to begin with. "Send it to the referring party." I signed the required papers and headed on my way.

I pulled myself together and called TJ at work.

"Hi, TJ. I finally found the surgeon. He's say's its risky, but he's willing to operate." TJ cheered as if we won the lottery, before becoming dead silent.

"Are you okay, my dear?"

"I'm going to be fine."

"How long do you have to wait for surgery?"

"Ten weeks."

"That's a long time to wait in your condition," TJ mentioned, with tension in his voice.

"I've been put on the cancellation list, but that doesn't guarantee anything."

"I realize that."

Later that night while I was resting, the phone rang. Dr. Jones, the emergency room doctor, wanted an update.

"Hi Laura, I'm calling to see how things are going."

"Dr. Kelly has scheduled me for surgery."

"That's good. Who referred you to him?"

"I thought it was you."

"It wasn't me. I've never heard the name before."

I closed my eyes and connected with my spirit guide. He had a huge smile on his face and the angel from the hospital standing right beside him.

"It must have been divine intervention."

"Are you feeling any better?"

"Relieved, but the pain is still bad."

"Remember, it's important to take the painkillers so the pain doesn't spiral out of control."

"I will."

"You sound upset tonight. Is there anything I can help you with?"

"I had a disturbing call from my family doctor's office. I was told nobody wanted to help me. The secretary went so far as to tell me that Dr. Jones didn't believe me either."

"That's a lie. I know exactly what's going on and where that originated from. That's the type of bullying we doctors face. How dare they do that to you? Laura, I never implied anything like that. I hope you believe me. I'm really sorry they treated you this way."

"Dr. Jones, I believe you. Thank you for everything you've done for me."

"Please stay within close proximity of a major hospital, until they have this clip removed."

"I'll try."

"If you need anything, call."

The weeks went by and my condition continued to worsen. One night TJ and I were watching TV and something funny came on. I started to laugh; within seconds I started bawling. The damn clip had moved yet higher.

The following day, x-rays were done to see how far it had travelled. Different x-ray technicians came in to check it out: "Oh wow, look at that!" "Does that hurt?" "Are you always aware of where it is?" "Holy shit, where'd that come from?"

I sat there falling apart inside, knowing this wasn't good. I felt like I was dying, which wasn't far from the truth. I was prepared to die, if things were stalled any longer.

I spent most of my time in bed or on the couch. I often struggled to find a comfortable position. I gradually lost my appetite. TJ spent more time taking care of me as I became sicker. I scaled back my readings. At times I'd break out coughing uncontrollably when I spoke, because of the height the clip had reached. I ended up falling ill at several book signings.

My last book signing ended off key. Earlier in the day, I had spent time enjoying my friend's adorable baby boy. He smiled when I bounced him up and down. He giggled when I held him high above my head. Then at the signing, I had a box under the table, in which I kept extra supplies. I bent down a few times to retrieve items from it. I spent most of the day in the front of the store greeting the customers as soon as they entered.

I stood chatting with two unique ladies at my signing, who had just bought my book. One of the ladies was handicapped and held a cane in each hand. The other was very well dressed and kept pumping me for information. Then tragedy struck mid-sentence like a bullet, when the clip suddenly shifted, lodging into my spleen. I stood, struggling to breathe, as my face turned red. I was leaned over my table and made it to my chair. I sat fighting back the tears that welled up in my eyes.

There was a hospital directly across the street, but one where I couldn't get help. That's where Dr. Mohammed practiced. The director of his hospital rejected me several weeks prior, refusing to hear me out. I'd been to the four other major city hospitals and was eventually ushered out.

I called TJ at work, telling him I couldn't breathe. While managing a noisy production line, he failed to fully tune into the disaster I was facing. "Laura, try to relax. You need to stay calm. You have ten days to go. You can do this. You're going to be fine. You have to wait for your surgery, because none of the doctors will help you. I'll see you at home when I get home. Dear, you'll be fine."

The lady with two canes, raced to get me water. The other lady kept talking as if nothing had changed. When I couldn't respond to her question, she became irate. She tore off in a hurry and marched though the exit gate. The courageous handicapped woman with the two canes emerged in a hurry. She handed me the water and looked into my face with concern and worry.

"Take a few sips dear," she was very calm and extremely understanding. "I'm sensing something seriously wrong deep inside you. That red bracelet on your wrist indicates that you've been matched for a blood transfusion. When is this surgery that you desperately need?"

"I'm booked for surgery in ten days to have a loose surgical clip removed that has just hit my spleen."

"Can you get a hold of this doctor and move the date ahead?"

"He's on holidays. The operation is booked for his first day back."

"Can you go to emergency?"

"They won't help me. I've already traveled the circuit."

"I hear you."

I sat there, crying in pain on a chair in the middle of a bookstore beside a stranger. Deep inside I realized in an instant that death could be my fate. I knew that I was in serious trouble and that I couldn't get the medical help I needed. Dr. Jones was in England. Dr. Kelly was in France. I bowed my head in prayer and took a chance.

I thanked God for the life I had already lived. I put in an urgent request for more time, if permitted. I connected with my guides requesting divine intervention. I asked the angels to watch over me and to keep me safe.

A flock of angels immediately appeared and gathered around. I sat watching them. They shifted my energy and lightened the burden. I bowed my head and thanked them for giving me the strength to survive.

"Thank you for being there for me." I said to the caring disabled woman. "I appreciate your help. I'm doing a little better now and I need to go home."

"Those angels that were in our midst lifted your pain."

"Yes, they did a great job. Again, thank you for your help. I need to leave." I quietly thanked the angels on my way out the door.

The next several days were extremely challenging. I spent most of my time in bed. TJ ended up taking care of everything.

Three days before my surgery, I found a new family doctor to receive my surgical report. I was shown this doctor through a vision several weeks before. She treated me with genuine respect and care.

"Laura," the kind pleasant woman spoke. "You're going to be okay. I'm here for you. Call me if you need anything."

Spirit kept showing me images related to the surgery over the next several nights. I was fairly cool with it until I was shown a large white bag beside my thigh. I became frightened, unsure of what I'd seen.

"TJ, are you awake?" I gently poked him in bed.

"Yes, dear. What do you need?"

"I'm scared. There's a large white bag on a stretcher beside my leg. It's so big the top reaches my hip. I sure hope I'm going to be okay."

"I think you're going to be fine. You weren't shown a body bag or a coffin."

"You have a point. Good night, TJ. I love you."

On the verge of falling asleep, the night before surgery, I was shown a gold colored silhouette of TJ kissing me on the forehead, as I lay on a stretcher.

In the morning I was a bundle of nerves. TJ sat with me while I waited to go into surgery. All necessary precautions were being taken. The large white bag I saw in a vision ended up being inflatable stockings. These were in a sealed bag beside my legs.

TJ stood at my side as various people showed up introducing themselves. Dr. Kelly had put together a highly qualified surgical team. There were four other doctors and five nurses present to assist him with my surgery.

Several months earlier, TJ was in my shoes and now the table was turned. Before TJ became ill, I awoke one morning and saw a yellow gallbladder with black polka dots. The word sick was printed on top of it.

TJ lacked energy and generally felt ill. I told him about what I'd seen and he readily dismissed it as belonging to someone else.

It wasn't until he became extremely ill that he bothered checking it out. A doctor's confirmation didn't set him straight. He waited until he saw an airbrushed message on my teenager, Mary's, television set. The drawing was of a gallbladder bursting and dripping with pus. Mary told him if she were him, she'd be getting to a hospital before it was too late.

Our first Valentine's Day as a married couple was spent in the emergency room saving TJ's life. He spent several days in the hospital to bring the infection under control before they could operate. TJ's gallbladder was within hours of bursting when they finally opened him up. Progressive visions of his operation were being revealed to me by Spirit, while he was in surgery. I knew from what I was shown that he was going to be okay.

TJ had surgery in February; I had mine in March, and here we were again in August, dealing with what should have happened back then. We both struggled with serious illnesses in our first year of marriage.

Dr. Kelly showed up at my side. "Laura, this surgery is going to be dangerous. If the situation becomes life threatening, I'm going to have to stop." He seemed very concerned and a little hesitant.

"Doctor Kelly, I understand." I lay there with tears streaming down my face.

"You're going to do okay. I love you." TJ gently squeezed my hand and kissed my cheek. "You'll be back before you know it."

A nurse started moving the stretcher towards the operating room. I started experiencing bouts of uncontrollable sobbing, which would come and go. Being completely stressed out, I forgot to mention the clip was residing in the spleen.

The surgical team was extremely pleasant and supportive in every way. They knew I was stressed. One of the nurses held my hand. A doctor lost a vein. He apologized and started searching for a better vein. Another doctor came over to introduce himself. They kept me talking until I went under.

I awoke in the recovery room, struggling to breathe through the searing pain. "You're okay. Breathe. I'm putting morphine into your line," I could hear a voice say. Then I heard a jar being rattled and the rustling of a plastic bag. I knew without a doubt the damn clip was out.

Dr. Kelly found TJ in the waiting room.

"TJ, your wife is doing well and the clip is out. The last part of her surgery got a little dicey. The clip had attached itself to her spleen. I had to carefully open the scar tissue on the spleen to remove it. There were no complications. Everything went fine. I'm sending her home with you today. They should be bringing her up shortly from recovery."

TJ leaned over the stretcher and kissed me on the forehead within seconds of me being wheeled into the room.

"Honey, I love you. They got the clip out. It was attached to your spleen. You're coming home with me today." I fell into a deep sleep some time shortly after.

A couple of hours later TJ drove us home. He was so overwhelmed that he grabbed my bag and left me in the car. I made it halfway around the front of the car. TJ realized something was up when our neighbor rushed towards me to help.

TJ stayed home the first week. Getting up was difficult with five fresh incisions. They went halfway through my body with laparoscopes. Two of the openings were below the navel and to the left. The larger one was inside the top of my belly button. The other two were several inches apart under the ribcage on the right side, on the opposite side of the spleen.

A lump the size of an egg formed above the incision near my navel. I had stopped taking the painkillers, because they irritated my stomach.

The pain escalated and spiraled out of control, and then complications set in. Seven days after surgery, I was sent back to the hospital by a very concerned doctor from a clinic. I was in so much pain that tears streamed down my cheeks. TJ became extremely irritated while driving me to the hospital.

"I thought when you had surgery, that was the last of all of this," he spoke, breaking the silence.

I was in so much pain that I needed to focus on my breathing. I knew he was frustrated, but so was I.

TJ sat across the cubicle from my stretcher in emergency repeatedly uttering "you deserve this," out loud to me, at least half a dozen times, in a loud firm snarky voice.

Morphine was administered, quickly bringing the pain under control. I silently wondered if the man I married was starting to reveal his true colours. I remember lying there seriously considering leaving him.

Shorty after, a porter showed up to whisk me off to x-rays. He stopped for something at the nurse's station, when an angel appeared. "Don't worry you're going to be okay," she said, smiling directly at me.

TJ told a nurse I had done this to myself by doing a load of laundry. My husband was still tender and recovering from his surgery, which had happened several months earlier. He was irritated knowing he had to be at a job he hated in less than eight hours. It took TJ a while to simmer down, after that he treated me much better.

Our washing machine is outside our bedroom door. I put my dirty clothes directly into the washer, one item at a time over several days. It was easier for me to do it that way, instead of using the hamper. The detergent sat on a shelf above the appliance. I reached and pressed the button which dispenses soap into a cup. I added it to the small load and started the machine. Later in the day I asked TJ to put the load in the dryer. He assumed that I lifted the hamper and dumped it into the washer.

After the pain was successfully controlled, one of the nurses informed us that everything checked out fine. She went on to tell us that the doctor was planning to release me, but he would be a while. A couple of hours later, we found out that the doctor we were waiting for was the only one working this busy city emergency room. We left on our own accord.

On the way home, TJ was in a better mood. He helped me into the house and we went straight to bed.

In the morning he called in to work and took the day off. This job was coming to an end anyways. Several months back, I called TJ at work. This call was answered in the most unusual manner. "This extension no longer exists," a voice from beyond warned. Immediately, I understood the situation, but TJ refused to accept it.

While convalescing in bed, I opened a letter from one of my clients which read:

Hi Laura,

I don't know if you remember me or not. I'm the mom with the sick baby. The doctors had told me he was going to die. And you said no he is going to be okay. I thought you must be wrong, since they were so sure. Well they were wrong and he is going to be fine. The said they were sorry for the stress. I know they made a mistake, so I am not upset, but I could not believe how wrong they were and that you knew.

You were right about them not telling us what was going on as well. I actually acted kind of crazy and went to the hospital and would not leave until they helped him. We stayed five days! I am not like that. I never second guess a doctor. I just could not handle seeing him suffer and no one caring.

Something was wrong. They just kept telling me they were going to look into things, but nothing happened. They actually said he was going to be a case study and they were all going to follow him closely. The next time they saw him they did not know who he was or bother reading his chart. They told me they could not help him and that he was dying and also that he would be moderately to profoundly retarded and not to have unrealistic expectations. (I talked about him being a normal boy.)

They kept increasing his medication without even looking at him. They increased it to the maximum dose, which put him in a fog. This medicine has a common side effect of blindness in more than a third of patients. If it had not been for what you said, I do not know if I would have had the courage to stick up for my son. This would have been terrible, since I am his only voice. I cannot believe the ripple effect you started. I hope someone else can be helped as well. Hope is a funny thing. I am so grateful. I was in such a dark place and when you said that, it really gave me hope.

But I thought it could not possibly be true.

He had several of their top field specialists look at him and they all agreed there was not much hope for him.

I would not have believed it if it had not happened to me. I hope his story will help others.

> *Thank you from the bottom of my heart, Jayne Peters*

Reading her letter boosted my spirits, even though I was bedridden and in severe pain. It took a while to recover after getting past a couple complications and setbacks, but eventually everything healed nicely.

My health has been completely restored, other than mild tenderness in the muscles around the ribcage. I'm no longer sick and all the symptoms are gone. For the first time in years my hair actually shines. It's been six months since the surgery and I'm still enjoying good health. All I need to do is lose some weight and rebuild weak muscles.

Unfortunately, there is no legal action being taken. The lawyers here are not interested in going up against these doctors. They have a variety of excuses such as: these doctors are going to fight; they're well known; too much time has passed; you were in a couple of bad car accidents; it's going to take years. If you're a lawyer and willing to take these people to task, by all means, please contact me.

"Suddenly I stood face to face with death. All I could see was a solid black silhouette of a head and neck. Death was neither male nor female. I wasn't scared, but curious. The Angel of Death slowly smiled at me···

A new spiritual awareness sets in for those who are close to death. People are unaware of the power and knowledge of the soul. Family members panic when loved ones speak of seeing the deceased...

Even though their earthshells have expired, their souls live on. The dead are appearing to loved ones to let them know that everything is okay. These visits repeatedly verify an afterlife, and Heaven's location seems to be a dimension away.

People fear through Biblical teaching that it's wrong to communicate with the dead. Is this really any different from Jesus appearing after his death? Many truths have been altered and hidden for the purpose of control."

- ***Laura Laforce***

Chapter 9

Lifting the Veil

"I'll never forget staring death in the face."

Unwinding after a busy day, a glimpse of my friend Trudy was revealed like a photo in a frame. Just 30 seconds later the image returned – with the taste of death. Grotesque coldness penetrated my solar plexus, sending chills up my spine. I knew that instant Trudy was going to die.

"Spirit, please don't take her," I bargained, hoping to be heard. "Is there any way her life can be spared? I need her. Why don't you take someone else instead?" My bald guide stood in my peripheral vision shaking his head in disbelief.

My elderly friend Trudy was hospitalized with double pneumonia. I knew her days were numbered, and our time together was coming to an end.

Numerous visions prepared me for certain future events. As each event occurred, time drew nearer. I was shown a covered body on a gurney near the elevator. Days later, I arrived at the hospital and the premonition unfolded before my eyes. I was relieved to find Trudy lying asleep in her bed. The deceased person in the hallway was a stranger who had met his demise.

This is something I should have known from past experience on a missing person's case. I had spent hours working on a delicate case. One night I received an upsetting image, which unfolded in a morgue. Workers moved around the room carrying out various tasks. A body was covered up to the forehead with a white sheet. The only part exposed was the corpse's mid-length black hair. Days later, a body was found, in the same area, where a person that I was looking for went missing. The body wasn't that of the victim I'd been searching for. The covering indicated a stranger.

I'd spent numerous hours at Trudy's side in Palliative Care. One afternoon her mother's spirit appeared beside the bed. Trudy briefly acknowledged her mother before falling asleep. Different orbs kept floating in and out of the curtains surrounding her bed. What shocked me the most is when she started negotiating with them out loud in her sleep. She'd nod her head in agreement just like she did with everybody else. I distinctly heard her say, "Time's almost up," nodding her head in agreement.

Trudy opened her eyes and looked directly at me. "Laura, can you do some of your healing work on me? Focus on my lungs. There so full of garbage that it's difficult to breathe."

I started working on her immediately. I called in the angels and her spirit guides. I was shown by her guides how to send and where to circulate the energy. A few minutes after I finished working on her, she vomited a large volume of dark yellow stuff. I rang the bell for help.

The nurse came rushing in to help. An expression of shock adopted her face. She immediately buzzed for more help. "Oh my," she stated, trying to cover her discomfort. "I bet you feel better. This isn't vomit. It's all the stuff that's been clogging your lungs. I've never seen a patient release it like this before." Heavy sticky mucus covered the front of Trudy's gown and most of her sheets. It took two nurses almost ten minutes to get her cleaned up. I excused myself while they tended to her and stepped outside her curtain.

I stood against the bedroom wall and looked in on her roommate Marge who was sound asleep. This poor woman suffered immensely. I always knew deep inside she'd be the first to go. I worried about this affecting Trudy. Dying people should have their own private rooms. Being in the same room, they affected each other's energy fields. Noisy machines surrounding Marge would kick in periodically, disturbing Trudy.

I remember the first time I met Marge. I stopped at the foot of her bed with a big smile on my face and said hello. She smiled in return with all the energy she could muster. What really struck me was the beauty of her soul. Her aura lit up, brightly radiating great joy. Marge could no longer communicate due to her rapidly deteriorating condition. There was something special about this lady. She seemed to have originated from the old country.

I closed my eyes and tried connecting with her spirit guide. Instantly, images of two young Russian girls were shown. They were skipping down dirty narrow roads, which ran between old decrepit buildings. Sounds of footsteps entering the bedroom brought me back. They stopped at the foot of Marge's bed. I heard gentle scraping as the drapes were pulled open and then slid shut.

"I really hate coming here. I don't understand her. I can talk with other patients, but this one shuts me out. I don't understand why she's still alive. Her useless children who hired me should be here instead; perhaps this is her problem with me."

"She shouldn't be with us much longer. Patients like her often die alone," the doctor sighed.

I quickly whipped open the drapes that separated us. "Excuse me ladies." The hired help frantically searched my face. A part of her conscience knew that her attitude was unacceptable.

"I was just venting," the offending woman huffed, trying to save face.

"Can I make a quick suggestion?" I offered, hoping my words wouldn't fall on deaf ears.

"Okay," the doctor answered while the snobbish helper beside her stood glaring at me.

"In the last days people need compassionate care. They deserve to be comforted and loved. I find it easier to express this through physical touch and closeness. Being with them makes a world of difference. Smile and make eye contact. Speak in a quiet gentle voice. Reach over and hold their hand or gently message their feet. When people are treated with love, it's easier for the soul to release."

"Thank you sharing this. I'm a new doctor." She reached over and gently held Marge's hand. Her tense patient immediately relaxed. "I can see exactly what you're talking about and this makes sense. Does this have something to do with energy?"

"Yes, the transfer of energy is why touch is useful and comforting."

"I see."

"I'd better get going. My meter's about to expire," the miserable aide swept up her purse and marched out of the room.

A short while later, a team of two therapists and a different doctor strutted into the room.

"Hi Marge, we're hear to check you out," one of techs shrieked at the top of her lungs.

I kept sensing Marge had a tragic past. She'd shut down immediately when strangers entered the room in order to protect herself.

"Marge is being stubborn. She isn't co-operating with us," the voice of the frustrated middle-aged male physician boomed. "You're making this a lot harder than it has to be," he harshly addressed the dying woman.

I came around to the opening in the curtain. "Stop treating Marge that way. Where's your respect? I can only imagine how you treat your mother."

"I'm behind on my rounds. She's holding up my schedule," he smoothly excused himself, trying to keep cool.

"You shouldn't be allowed to work with ill people. You're abusing this dying woman. If I ever hear you treating patients like this again, I'll report you."

He and his followers quickly finished examining her and left the room.

I quietly went over to Marge and gently placed my hand on her foot.

"Marge, are you okay?" She nodded her head and lightly moaned. I tried to send her some healing energy to help ease her pain.

"I'm sorry they treated you that way. Do you need anything?" She remained quiet and fell into a deep sleep.

"Angels, please watch over Marge," I whispered, while trying to send her healing comfort. Still standing at her feet with my eyes shut, I was interrupted by an intruding vision.

Darkness was manifesting at the nurses' station. Something negative was going on. I quietly slipped out of the room and strolled close enough to the unit desk to catch wind of what was going down.

"You ladies are to concentrate on caring for Helen Brown and Randy Bausch. Let the other patients fend for themselves," the cold hearted nurse ordered.

"Excuse me," a young woman's high-pitched voice piped up. "That's not right. We have more than two patients here. What about the others?"

"They're dying and they don't matter."

"We're supposed to help people, not ignore them."

"I got orders from administration this afternoon to trim hours. We'll have a lot less time to devote to the patients."

"Those two patients you named are no better off than the others. They're also dying."

"They are the two most likely to cause us issues if they're not cared for. The Bausch's run a huge business. They donate thousands to this hospital every single year," the charge nurse rattled. "Tell you what. Instead of cutting hours, I'm terminating you for insubordination. You're dismissed as of now. Grab your things and leave."

I carried on past the desk appearing oblivious to what had just occurred. I stood by the elevators waiting for the nurse who been fired. I pushed the down button when I saw her walk towards me. An empty elevator opened and both of us quietly entered.

"I heard what happened," I quietly addressed the teary eyed woman who stared directly ahead.

"If you need a witness, I'm available." I handed the speechless woman my business card.

After supper, I returned to the unit. Marge's airbed lay empty in the hall. She died while I was out. I took a seat beside Trudy.

"Marge is gone."

"I know. I saw her bed in the hallway on the way back. How are you handling this?"

"I'm okay. That poor lady really suffered," Trudy said.

We watched a bright orb dart across the room several times before stopping to hover in front of us.

"We have a visitor," Trudy piped up.

"Marge has come back from Heaven to say good-bye." We both acknowledged Marge and she disappeared from sight.

"Laura, I'm thirsty. Could you grab my drink?"

I held Trudy's glass to her lips as she took a few sips. I sat with her until visiting hours were over, then left for home.

On the way home, I reminisced about the good times we'd shared. Our friendship was close despite the 30-year age gap. We met shortly after she became a widow and I a divorcee. Trudy and I played the field and compared notes. We prided ourselves on our shared nickname Cougaress.

We both found lovers at the same time and fell head over heels in love. Both guys dumped us without saying good-bye. We sat crying over them like spilt milk, piecing our lives back together. Now death was stepping between us.

Unwinding that evening seemed impossible. Too much had gone on during the day. My office seemed to be the perfect refuge. I sat down at the computer and started working on my book. I started adding that day's events into the story. Random numbers suddenly hit my screen one by one. I looked down at my keyboard making sure my fingers weren't displaced. I attempted to delete the mysterious numbers. An invisible force instantly pulled my keyboard away then closed the moveable drawer it rested on.

"Hey, stop that! Give my stuff back. I need it," I demanded out loud. I felt a heavy presence lurking in the room.

"What's happening over there?" TJ interrupted, "I feel a strong presence."

"Someone is controlling my computer and entering a series of digits. It's even pulled away my keyboard and pushed my desk tray away."

TJ leaned back in his chair hoping to catch some of the action. "Whoever this is wants your attention," he said, rolling his chair towards me with a grin on his face.

The invisible force re-entered the same numbers. It was a series of five numbers. These were serial numbers "00665" morphed into an inked tattoo on a pale forearm. An image invaded my vision of Marge dressed in office attire typing on an old fashioned typewriter. This retired secretary was a holocaust survivor. After this episode, Marge vanished into thin air. This explained her reactions to various staff members that she encountered.

I tossed and turned that night in bed. I found it difficult to sleep. Trudy kept materializing. There is a fine veil between the living and the dead. Sometimes, when people are unconscious or deathly ill, they can mimic ghosts. A few times I'd wondered if she'd passed, but I hoped she was still with us. I wasn't ready to lose her yet.

I sat sobbing on the couch at three in the morning. My abdomen extended with inflammation making the pain almost unbearable. Trudy kept showing me two letter "X's" in reference to my physical pain. She revealed the hand of a surgeon. Then she disappeared. Trudy showed up again and sent me an image of myself backstage in a fancy light purple dress. Then she shared what I understood to be her last breath. I broke down bawling. Before I could pull myself together TJ was at my side comforting me.

"What's wrong?" TJ asked, trying to console me as he wiped away the tears.

"I saw Trudy die. She was sleeping and breathing weirdly. Suddenly her eyes opened and hit the back of her head three times." My body shook with intensity making my other issues worse.

"And then what?" TJ was trying to figure out exactly what was going on.

"Then, I don't know. It probably means she's dead."

The following afternoon, the ordeal played out identically to what I'd been shown. I sat beside my friend, helplessly watching her go through the motions, with tears welling in my eyes. Her eyes hit the back of her head three times. She struggled to inhale. Suddenly a nurse's voice interrupted, crackling over the intercom above her bed. This snapped her out of the state she'd entered. Talk about being saved by the bell!

Two foreign janitors started arguing outside her room. They were so loud I ended up shutting her door, allowing her the peace and privacy she deserved if she was going to pass.

I brought up the occurrence during a conversation several days later. Trudy immediately recalled the entire event. She'd been watching it herself from the ceiling.

"Next time I start dying, would you grab my leg or foot and shake me. I'm not ready to die. It's not my time to go. I have many things that need to be sorted out. Besides, I wouldn't be in this condition if the doctors had done their jobs. They repeatedly came up with conflicting misdiagnoses. They refused to address my situation until it was almost too late. I kept telling them that the medicine they were giving me was making me worse. They went ahead and doubled the dose and put the damned stuff through my IV. While dozing off, I overheard one the nurses say, 'Patients like her drain our blood supply,' while hanging a fresh unit of blood."

"That's awful. Don't listen to them. You deserve blood just as much as anyone else. This is why we try to make sure one of us is always around for you."

We had numerous problems with the hospital. I can recall coming in to visit. The moment I arrived a staff member was removing her untouched lunch tray. I immediately grabbed the meal back and started feeding Trudy her lunch. She was too weak to feed herself. After lunch I approached the head nurse.

"Why aren't you making sure the patients are eating? Trudy is too weak to fend for herself. If I hadn't dropped in, this wouldn't have been good for her."

"We try our best, but we can't help them all. This is why it's important for family to be involved."

"Family and friends are involved. Someone didn't show up when they were supposed to and nobody was notified. Would you at least have the courtesy to make sure someone is with her?" I firmly requested before going back to Trudy.

"Laura, did you report that young physiotherapist who got angry with me this morning for being too weak to stand beside the bed, the one that told me if I kept it up I'd never walk again?"

"That's awful Trudy; I'll mention her to the nurses before I leave."

"Did I tell you that in the middle of the night, I rang my bell six times trying to get help? I was forced to lie in my shit, in the same position, for over two hours. They were short staffed and dealing with a crisis. A lady down the hall got out of bed and smacked her head wide open on the nightstand. Her disabled roommate kept buzzing and screaming. By the time staff arrived, the woman was dead on the floor."

"That's horrible. None of these things should ever be allowed to happen." Trudy and I spent the remainder of the day reminiscing about the good things we enjoyed together.

That afternoon I sprung a surprise on her. I draped her tray table with a lacy table cloth. I pulled out china tea cups and fancy desert plates.

"Oh, this is beautiful. Just like old times." Her whole demeanor changed to utter happiness.

I draped her with a fancy scarf and whipped out my camera. "Trudy, smile." I hit the wall backing up trying to get the best angle possible. I snapped several pictures. Just before I finished, a nurse walked in.

"It's nice to see you ladies enjoying your visit. Let me know if you need anything," the nurse attentively offered, taking in the interesting display.

"Could you please take a few photos of us together?" I asked.

"Sure, I'd be glad to."

I made my way to the head of the bed and put my arms around my frail friend. "Cougaress, smile on three."

We thanked the nurse for helping us and proceeded with our tea party. I opened my thermos of steaming hot water and dropped in the teabags. We sat taking in the afternoon sunrays, enjoying homemade brownies and freshly brewed peppermint tea. We watched and talked about the different orbs that were floating by.

"Last night my old neighbors were standing beside my bed. I couldn't understand why they dropped in. They've both been dead for well over twenty years. I wasn't close to them. I used to babysit their children," Trudy mentioned, trying to make sense of the event.

"Perhaps you meant more to them than they did to you."

"I get it; just like the guys we used to love."

"Yes it was something like that, but without the heartbreak," I said before gradually tearing myself away. "I really enjoyed spending the day with you. Try to get some rest. I love you."

"I love you too, and God Bless," she said, squeezing my hand. "Good-bye and come back soon."

Shortly after arriving home, I drew a bubble bath. A sweet lilac fragrance filled the steamy air. I took my time as I immersed myself into the suds. Relaxing from the tension of the day, I started recalling how different things were at this time last year. It was only a year ago that Trudy was preparing to give the eulogy at a close friend's funeral and now we were preparing to say good-bye. I remember her being stressed over the presentation she was about to make. We spent time going over it until she felt it was perfect. Before she left for the funeral, she was worried about keeping her composure. Now I completely understood where she was at. Only this time, I was about to wear the shoes of the survivor.

In the morning I awoke to the sight a grey life-size set of lungs. The plagued organ literally hung in my face before my sleep laden eyes. TJ lay sprawled across his side of our bed.

"TJ, you awake?" I didn't want to disturb him, but I really need to talk.

"Yes, dear. What do you need?" TJ rolled onto his side and put his arm around me.

"I just saw grey-filled lungs. Something's wrong with Trudy. I need to see her right away before it's too late. Visiting with people after they've died is never the same."

"Are you going to head out soon?" my husband inquired, reaching over to switch off the alarm clock before it buzzed.

"I'll leave right after breakfast." I started grabbing random clothes from the closet. I was in too much of a frenzy to be selective. "Remember we sensed Trudy being with us a couple of days ago," I reminded him while handing him a fresh cup of brew in his favorite mug.

"She partially materialized in front me. Then she looked me directly in the eye."

"Trudy sure gets around," TJ added, pulling out his kitchen chair.

"She always has." I stood at the counter fixing my coffee to my liking.

"One night last week she was in our bedroom watching us."

"Oh my God, what were we doing?" TJ sputtered, almost choking on his morning coffee.

TJ's reaction was priceless. I purposely stalled before answering him. "You were sleeping."

"Oh, thank God." A sigh of relief could be

"That's not as bad as what she did to me."

"What happened?" TJ was eager to hear the rest. He put his coffee mug on the table. He gently grabbed the edge of the kitchen table bracing himself. "Tell me!"

I contemplated letting him suffer in order to save myself from embarrassment.

"She popped in on me when I was taking a shower," I mentioned in a calm sincere voice.

"That must have been awkward," TJ sympathized while pushing himself away from the table.

"It wasn't as bad as when my aunt appeared to me while I was bathing."

"I don't know why you get all the good stuff. Don't you think it's a little unfair?" TJ said, adjusting his collar.

"You know that the very ill are capable of leaving their bodies. They spend time visiting loved ones or checking out the other side." I stood looking in the mirror teasing my stubborn hair into place.

"The last time I visited her at the hospital, I told her our bedroom and bathrooms were off limits."

"How did she take that?" A look of curiosity sparked in his eyes.

"Trudy said she was worried about me. She was trying to figure out how to help remove the nasty bullet before she died." I started applying my gooey mascara to my lower lashes. I struggled with the idea of losing her. "TJ, I'm ready to go. I'll see you when I get back."

"Say hi to Trudy for me. Tell her I love her," TJ said, walking me to the door and kissing me good-bye.

The drive to town seemed to take an eternity. Eventually I arrived at the hospital. Approaching her bedroom, I felt something was very wrong. The energy seemed distorted. One of her nurses stopped me in the hallway.

"Before you go in, you'll need gown up, put on a mask and gloves."

"What's wrong?" I needed to understand what I was facing.

"She's in isolation. She's come down with a superbug. The droplets she expels are highly contagious and resistant to antibiotics."

This created tension in me, but I wasn't going to allow this nasty bug to interfere.

"How's she doing?"

"Not bad. She hasn't been out of bed today."

I stood in the hallway figuring out the yellow gown. I felt a wave of anxiety hit. This situation pushed me beyond my comfort zone. Getting sick was the least of my worries. I was concerned about the condition Trudy would be in. I took a deep breath and walked into her room. She looked horrible, like a living skeleton with flesh.

Hey, Cougaress, it's Laura. How do you like my new attire?" Her face beamed with joy. I stood quietly assessing the new situation. They had put her on an airbed, just like Marge. An image took over showing Trudy's head cocked to the side. A hand shut Trudy's eyelids for the last time. Wearing the mask was easier than I had originally thought. It probably blocked my facial reaction to the horrifying presentation.

"It's smashing and provocative. Better not let the guys see you dressed like that. They'll run like hell. Mr. Mike says he can no longer see me. He refuses to dress up to visit."

"He's just scared."

"Of what?"

"Looking sexy."

"Why don't you lower your mask? Pull it up when the staff come by. That way you won't sound so muffled?"

"I'd love to, but I can't afford to catch this. How about I sit closer instead?" Everything had changed overnight. Her energy was lower.

"Can you please do some healing work on me?" she politely asked, hoping I'd oblige her. "Concentrate on my eyes. It would be nice to see my surroundings. The rest of my body is rather hopeless." Just as I thought, she was fading. The eyes are the window to the soul. She was dying and her eyes were shutting down.

"Okay, let's do some color therapy and healing together. Are you ready to start?"

"Yes."

I stood at the foot of her bed cupping one foot in each of my hands. I grounded myself before starting. "Close your eyes with me. I want you to only watch the color swirls that you see with your eyes shut." I immediately invited the angels and her guides to help. Bright beams of light started to appear. "Trudy do you see the bright yellow lights?"

"Yes."

"They're angels. Look at them. Aren't they beautiful? Look directly at the green healing light they're sending you."

"Oh, that's beautiful."

We enjoyed the moment together, watching the light show.

"Open your eyes, Trudy. Tell me how they are!"

"Everything is so much brighter. I can actually see the face of the clock. It's almost two o'clock."

"Sounds like they did what you needed."

I quietly shut my eyes with my hands still on her feet. Suddenly I stood face to face with death. All I could see was a solid black silhouette of a head and neck. Death was neither male nor female. I wasn't scared, but curious. The Angel of Death slowly smiled at me in a gentle sincere manner. The energy radiating from this spirit was warm and inviting. I instantly felt at ease. The perfect white teeth looked absolutely stunning against the ebony head. I opened my eyes and shut them again to discover Death had disappeared.

I spent longer visiting with Trudy. I realized time was drawing nearer. Death was waiting for her. I knew every moment was precious and now was what mattered. I hoped we'd have more visits, but I didn't know for sure. I made sure we enjoyed spending our time together.

"I really enjoyed it when you brought me Chinese food before Christmas. I wish we could sit in my dining room and enjoy all the tasty dishes again. We had a bit of everything and lots left over. Remember the beautiful flowers on the table and the glistening china we ate from? My fortune cookie was hilarious, stating I'd have the ultimate romance."

"It was perfect. Laughing over the cookies made our day."

"Those days are gone and I'm stuck here. Who would imagine life would come to this?" Her whole attitude shifted. She allowed her resentment to surface. "I don't know what I ever did to deserve being sick like this. I was a good person. I worked hard. I was a mother and a wife. I helped other people. I watch what I ate. I went to church. I loved to dance. And now I can't even get out of bed. What the hell's up with that?"

"Life isn't fair."

"Who'd imagine that my life would end up like this?"

I stayed longer, trying to cheer her up. I felt badly for her, but this unfortunate illness was out of our control. Perhaps this is part of her life plan, but I wasn't going there with her. I was losing my friend and she was losing her life. After Trudy calmed down, she became tired and wanted to sleep.

"Trudy, you need your rest. I'm going home. I love you, and remember; you mean the world to me." I felt tears welling in my eyes and she didn't need this.

"I love you too, dear. God bless you and keep you well."

"Thank you. May the angels watch over you and God keep you near."

I hugged her and brushed my gloved hand through her hair. I left her room and felt like I was falling to pieces, as I started to remove the protective lawyers. I pulled the gloves inside out from the wrist. I removed the mask and then the gown and disposed of them in the bins supplied. I tasted the scent of death throughout the rest of the day.

I awoke in the early morning hours out of a sound sleep. Trudy was smiling at me from the foot of our bed. Before I could say a word she lip-synched "Love you" and blew me a kiss good-bye before vanishing. I lay there teary-eyed with no doubt in my mind that she was gone.

By mid-morning I received a call from a family friend verifying what I already knew. This friend was the same person I'd seen in a premonition. She briefly mentioned a funeral was being planned for Trudy and that it would probably take place the following weekend. I tried hinting that a week day would be a better time to hold her celebration of life.

I had a huge out-town-event that weekend which I was not able to cancel. I struggled with the idea of not attending her funeral. Trudy and I visited numerous times since she had crossed over. She wouldn't have wanted me to cancel everything for her. Trudy wanted me to be successful and happy more than anything else.

Just as the conversation with the caller ended, Trudy's spirit was in my office. I felt her presence gently massaging the back of my neck. My head felt a little light with the exchange of energy, but I knew everything was alright. TJ was sitting in the room with me and started feeling a presence.

"Trudy's here," interrupted TJ with excitement.

"I know, she's been massaging the back of my neck."

After a while I retreated to our quiet bedroom alone. I wanted to link up with Trudy. I wanted the goods delivered firsthand. Before I opened my big mouth, Trudy was already present. She started off by sending me a vivid light show. I could see green grass and the outlines of buildings in the distance. She kept showing me her that her eyes were perfect; she could finally see again.

"Trudy, give me something for the readers." She knew about this book, which she was very proud of. Out of the blue I heard a tiny knock on the wall. "No, Trudy. Something bigger and better."

My cell phone suddenly rang. This totally interrupted everything and really pissed me off. I quickly answered the phone with a "Hello."

"Good-bye," spoke Trudy right into my ear. Before I could reply, she was gone without a trace.

Early in the evening, I heard an interesting tidbit from a friend relating to Trudy's death. A nurse had brought in her supper and sat the tray in front of her. While talking, she informed Trudy that a bed was found for her in a long term facility. Trudy lost it and snapped at the nurse, "I'm not going. I'd rather be dead." The caregiver left the room and returned fifteen minutes later and Trudy was gone. Her face was blue. She had choked to death.

Later that evening, a disturbance in my open pantry caught my attention. The folded metal stepping stool, which had previously leaned against the wall, was now vibrating out of control. I stood witnessing this poltergeist in action. An invisible entity applied pressure to the ladder, forcing the top rung into place, and then the thick bottom step was pushed into place.

An apparition of my late friend Trudy took a seat on the top step. She sat pleasantly smiling.

"Well hello, intruder. Identify yourself." I joked out loud, waiting for her response. I was aching to see how far she'd go. "Please don't write on the walls. We're trying to sell our house."

"Cougaress," was drawn in mid-air. Trudy remembered our shared nickname, which originated from our cougar days.

"Why don't you join me at the table – like old times?"

I went and sat in my chair. I looked over to the pantry and Trudy had disappeared.

Seconds later, she sat across from me like she used to. In life, she was a sophisticated gal with pizzazz. In death, she wasn't much different, except her body was more of a thin sheer apparition of who she used to be.

Trudy manifested a monochrome tea cup out of thin air and brought it to her pursed lips.

"Wait for me. Let's have tea together." I always had tea brewing at this hour and she knew it. I took a couple of seconds to pour a fresh cup. Trudy sat quietly watching me from the table.

I returned immediately with my own cup. We sat together sipping silently exchanging glances. My only frustration was that she no longer spoke like she used to. We communicated through telepathy and imagery.

"You seem fine. What do you do with all your time?" She smiled and nodded. Trudy pulled a tube of monochrome lipstick from thin air and applied it to her lips.

Trudy was the lipstick queen and clearly still is. She blew me a kiss and lip-synched "Love you," then vanished.

Trudy went to Janet's place and joined her at the table. Then she went to Sandra's home and switched her lights on and off. Next she went to Kelsey's and gently slid two hanging pictures to the floor.

Shortly after I left for groceries, Trudy paid TJ a visit. "Hello," she said in a very distant voice, followed by the sound of two footsteps.

A new spiritual awareness sets in for those who are close to death. People are unaware of the power and knowledge of the soul. Family members panic when loved ones speak of seeing the deceased. People are fearful when apparitions of living loved ones appear to them. Patients with Alzheimer's spend most of their time in the spiritual world gradually cutting themselves off from our reality.

Even though their earthshells have expired, their souls live on. The dead are appearing to loved ones to let them know that everything is okay. These visits repeatedly verify an afterlife, and Heaven's location seems to be a dimension away.

People fear through Biblical teaching that it's wrong to communicate with the dead. Is this really any different from Jesus appearing after his death? Many truths have been altered and hidden for the purpose of control.

Chapter 10

Children of the Light

My new client Alexia was at the door within minutes of her appointment. I led her to the table and made sure she was comfortable before we started. I'd seen the essence of her toddler close by. I knew this mother was hurting very deep inside.

"Alexia, your daughter is here."

The poor mother broke down bawling immediately. I allowed her the space to do what she needed.

"I feel guilty that she's gone. Had I been a better mother, she'd still be alive."

Alexia's guide was standing there shaking her head.

"This isn't your fault Alexia," I told her.

"But if I would have taken her to the doctor a day earlier, she might still be alive," Alexia replied.

The word "Leukemia" was spelled in midair by her guide.

"Your daughter had leukemia. It isn't your fault she's dead."

"I had dreams of her dying the week before, but I thought they were only nightmares."

"Lots of people have dreams like this," I explained. "It doesn't mean we can save the people we love."

"I sat at the hospital with her when she was dying," she continued. "I pushed my husband away the night I sensed her going. I wanted to be the only one with her when she went. Just like I was when she was born. I felt helpless and stressed. I went outside for a smoke and I offered my baby to God in a prayer. When I got back, I climbed into bed beside her and snuggled against her tiny little body. I wanted to be close to her.

"Out of exhaustion, I fell asleep. Lizzie and I held hands and we entered a dark foggy tunnel together. Hands were reaching out towards us through the thick fog. I kept hearing distorted voices calling out. Then we saw a very bright light at the end of the tunnel. My daughter skipped beside me, holding my hand and singing her favourite song. I bent down and told her that she was always my angel and I loved her very much. Then I kissed her good-bye for the very last time. An angel was in the tunnel holding out loving hands. I told Lizzie to go with the angel and she ran straight into her open arms. My Lizzie turned back and waved to me, looking over her shoulder with a huge smile on her face. "Good-bye, Mommy. I'm going to Heaven." My little darling disappeared into the bright light with an angel at her side.

"I awoke shortly after with tears in my eyes and looked at my little Lizzie. Her chest was no longer moving and I couldn't hear her breathe. I wasn't sure at first if I'd been dreaming. It all seemed surreal. Being unable to deal with reality, I rang for a nurse. All I was able to ask was, 'Is my Lizzie gone?' In a moment, the nurse told me, 'yes.' I knew I had brought my little girl over to God myself."

The distraught mother drew a breath.

"The rest of the family came up to the hospital to spend time. Her five year old brother Johnny climbed up on the bed to see his sister one last time. He kept asking me if she was really dead. He wanted to know exactly where she was. He sadly looked at me and got down on the floor to play. Being distraught, I was lost in my own world. I didn't notice that he had made his way back onto her bed. He lay at her feet and fell asleep. I briefly wondered why he was so quiet. I turned around and he was as still as Lizzie. I started shaking him to arouse him, which was unusually difficult. Eventually he came around and I took him off her bed. I explained to him he couldn't lie with his sister, because she was dead."

'Mommy, I went to see Lizzie. She was walking on a path, holding hands with a man in a robe that looked like Jesus, but I couldn't see his head or his hair. I wanted to go with her, but they told me no, it wasn't my time yet. They wouldn't let me stay in Heaven. They made me come back. Mom, that's not fair that she gets to stay up there.'

"Lizzie is an angel now and that's where they live. Heaven is for the people who can no longer live in their earthshells. This is what I told him, hoping he would understand. Lately Johnny's been having trouble adjusting and this is concerns me. He keeps talking about playing with his sister and acts as if they're hanging out together."

"Alexia, your daughter does come over to play with him. Your son isn't making any of this up." Lizzie was standing beside her mom waiting to be acknowledged.

"This can't be healthy for him."

"These visits he's having with his sister are normal and healthy. She also comes to you, but you haven't noticed."

"Tell me."

"She turns on the wind-up music box with the red roses on top of your dresser."

"I thought that was just a fluky thing."

"She made the baby monitor sound like a heartbeat. She says you got mad and threw it out."

"Oh my God, I feel terrible. I was so stressed after losing her that I figured there was something wrong with it. I pitched it and bought a new one for her baby sister's room.

I'm so terrified of losing another child that I've become overprotective. Is she angry that I threw it out?"

"Alexia, she loves you. She's not angry. She's a young child. She reaches out through play."

"Tell her I love her." The young mother burst into tears. "Talk to her the same way you always did."

Lizzie floated up beside her mother's face in a tiny beam and kissed her on the cheek, then vanished into thin air.

"Alexia, did you feel the warm pressure on your right cheek just now?"

"Yes, that was unusual. What was going on?"

"Lizzie just kissed you."

Alexia sat there quite overwhelmed, yet relieved. "I felt this before, but I didn't know what it was. So she's been trying to visit me and I never noticed or understood. What sort of mother am I anyways? I couldn't keep my child alive and I didn't pay attention to her when she came to visit me. You know I should have died instead. None of this is right."

"This anger and grief you're feeling right now is very normal. You didn't do anything wrong. Lizzie still loves you and she always will."

Alexia thanked me for helping. We exchanged hugs before she stepped out the door. No sooner had she pulled away, another frantic couple had called TJ and were on their way.

A short while later, I opened the door to a distraught couple.

"Hi Laura, we have an appointment with you."

I invited them to have a seat at the kitchen table. A teenaged boy around sixteen years of age appeared. He stood there waving at me to get my attention before he wrote Jordan in midair.

"Jordan is here to say hi to Mom and Dad," I started, allowing the information to flow.

His parents looked shocked, yet relieved. The couple sat, with tears in their eyes.

Jordan started showing me a horrific car accident. He was the driver and three other friends were in the car with him. He was the only one who didn't survive the crash.

"Your son Jordan shows me he died in a terrible car crash. He tells me he was the only one who didn't survive. He knows he's been forgiven for totaling the family car. He's been earthbound, because he never had the chance to say good-bye. He wants me to tell you both that he loves you very much. He's been doing things to be noticed."

"Oh, my God, that's our Jordan. Is he okay?" his mother interrupted, breaking into tears.

One of my gerbils started thumping her feet in terror from her cage in the corner. I turned my head just in time to see the apparition of Jordan attempting to touch her through the bars.

"Jordan, she's scared. Please let her be." I telepathically spoke to him to avoid any backlash from his parents. Seconds later he appeared, standing behind his father with monochrome remote controls. He proudly held one in each hand.

"Your son has been challenging you for the television set since he's been gone."

"He's a bit of a bad ass, but I have him beat. I watch the TV with two remote controls instead of one."

"Yes, I know, but he also has access to the two as well. He is standing behind you with both of them in his hands." I warned his father.

"He shows me that he opens up the garage door after you've closed it for the evening. He has started up your car and left it in running on the driveway."

"Yeah, I know. I almost run out of gas because of him. Yesterday was the anniversary of his death. He started a fire in a damp fire pit to mark the occasion. We enjoy his company, but ask him to think about safety."

"All you have to do is tell him in plain English. He can hear you perfectly well."

"Mom, he loves your collection of angels, even though he used to complain about the way they used to be organized."

"Oh my God, I thought that was him. That little bugger scared the hell out of me. We came back from holidays when I discovered every single angel had been moved and repositioned. The bigger angels were moved to the middle and they were arranged according to color and size. It looked as if an interior decorator had gotten a hold of them. The pink-haired angel in a flimsy lacy dress was missing. I later found her lying on her side at the bottom of the cabinet with her head pointed to the corner face down. Can you ask him why?" His mother sat waiting for an answer.

"He says she was a disgrace to the angels."

"When he was alive he always said she was ugly."

"Teenagers certainly have a way of saying things."

"I'm glad that he's here. We've been really missing him. Tell him that I love him," his mother told me, holding back her tears.

"Tell him yourself the same way you told me."
"Jordan, I love you and I always will."

"I love you son, I always have," his father piped up, grabbing at the chance. "Sorry I interrupted. I wanted the chance to say good-bye in case he left."

"That's alright." Jordan looked at them and waved good-bye blowing them a kiss, which morphed into a hollow pink heart. "He's saying good-bye. He wants you to know that he loves you both. He just sent you a pink floating heart. He's leaving now for the other side." Jordan turned away and walked, disappearing into the light.

"You know, it's a year since he's been gone," His mother was fighting back her tears.

"I can't get past the mourning. What do you suggest?"

"In time, things will get easier, but this deep longing never goes away. You'll find different ways of coping after a while. There is no right or wrong way to mourn and no set length of time. Remember him through the special times you shared. Hang up your favorite photos of him. Participate in the things you used to do together. Keep his memory alive."

Our bodies, or earthshells, are vessels that contain our souls. It's amazing how a mother can bring a child to the light. It's astounding that a young boy can follow his sister to the other side. She still comes to play with him even though she has passed. A dead son interrupts his parents to gain attention on a daily basis. Being able to communicate with deceased loved ones is natural. There is nothing sinful about it.

Chapter 11

Awakening of the Souls

Catastrophes and natural disasters sweep the entire earth. Terrorism lurks around the globe. Devastating recessions hit every single country. Millions starve to death living in substandard conditions. People face diversity fearing for their lives. Greed and corruption have taken the world by surprise. Society is reconnecting for survival through life altering events.

One morning I received a vision warning of trouble. Two indigo blue lakes were revealed, with the smaller one being surrounded by thick black smoke. The larger body of water was located further north. These lakes seemed to be somehow connected, but not physically. Another warning followed of a small adjacent town being on fire. Capital letters "S" and "L" were marked below the image.

Breaking news hit several hours later that the Town of Slave Lake was on fire. There are two Slave Lakes in Alberta; Greater and Lesser. A forest fire spiraled out of control at the smaller of the two. A state of emergency was declared and an entire town was evacuated. In a short period of time, half the town was engulfed in flames, destroying the homes it touched.

The following evening, a panic-ridden woman sat across the table from me. We joined hands and I shut my eyes before starting her session. My client's spirit guide showed her watching in horror as her house burned to the ground. "You watched your home burn to the ground." I started her reading. The stunned woman sat quietly with tears welling in her eyes. "You lost everything."

"Why does God let these bad things happen to good people? I feel so thankful to be alive, but so angry at the losses we suffered." She sat blotting the tears from her eyes with a tissue.

"This fire was an unfortunate event that contained extremely valuable life lessons."

"How could you say such a thing? Many people lost their houses." She almost became unhinged staring at me.

"Your loved ones survived. People in your community will share a special bond. This tragedy will bring a new awareness and respect toward each other."

"I had a premonition of our house being on fire, the day before this happened," she said. "Isn't that odd?"

"Not really. Premonitions and déjà vu provide glimpses of pre-existing knowledge that we're here to experience. We plan our lives and choose our lessons on the other side before coming here."

"Is this the same with other natural disasters?"

"Yes, we agree to participate in these horrific events to experience the emotions of tragedy."

"I never thought about it that way, but it makes sense. Thank you for your time." She appeared relieved before leaving the house.

Our world is not ending, although there are some difficult times to come. Souls of the living are awakening in order to survive. A gradual shift of awareness is upon us, bringing about positive changes over the next decade.

Chapter 12

Clarity through Connection

Valuable information is sent and received from beyond. The veil between the living and the dead is being lifted. People are learning to reconnect through the simplicity of love. Loving people have healthy boundaries, where hurt doesn't serve a purpose. I heard an unfamiliar voice declare; "Love, Endure and Evolve," three weeks before my wedding. I lay awake all night trying to decipher the message. I wondered what was wrong. Instead of enjoying the days leading up to our wedding, I was beside myself, extremely overwhelmed, I almost called off the wedding. These very words with the identical voice were delivered during a speech given at our reception

I awoke in the early morning hours beside TJ in the honeymoon suite. Two huge flashcards appeared near the ceiling with golden block sized capital letters reading "TJ" "HIM." Spirit relieved me, verifying that I married the right man.

We arrived at the front desk of the hotel to check out. I stepped up to the counter with TJ beside me and began to address the desk clerk. "My X and I," unconsciously flowed right out of mouth. I stepped back, horrified with the words which escaped. I spent days stressed out, analyzing the meaning of this phrase. Spirit verified through my own voice, that I had found my "X," in other words my soulmate, not ex-husband.

Three weeks after our wedding, intimacy abruptly came to a halt. Resentment and anger set in each time TJ refused me. I'd spend half the nights lying awake frustrated. After several weeks I harshly addressed my guide in the early morning hours. "Spirit, how dare you allow this to happen to me? I expected a loving romantic marriage with benefits. If I wanted celibacy I would have joined the convent. Why is this happening to us?" My guide appeared, smiling at me before vanishing into thin air.

Two mornings later, I awoke to a vision of a yellow pus filled organ with black dots plastered all over it and "sick" printed on top of the image in thick black letters. This was the most bizarre display I had ever received. This image looked like a liver, but who did this belong to? TJ never drank, so this must have been someone else's.

"Spirit, I don't understand this vision. How could it possibly pertain to our romantic situation?" Six months later, TJ fell ill and his gallbladder almost burst.

In our first year of marriage we faced extreme challenges and limited romance. There were times that I didn't know how we'd get through another day. Both of us faced life-threatening medical issues. Both of us had major surgery and suffered financial setbacks.

Being sensitive, I struggled with some of TJ's reactions towards me. I remember being so angry one night that I couldn't sleep. My spirit guide sang the word "love," repeatedly displaying the word on the bedroom ceiling and around all the walls. I lay there asking if I should leave TJ. One of my guides shook her head no. "Love" was the word she sent instead. This answer from beyond brought us closer together, saving our relationship.

Being connected brings clarity, keeping the guesswork out of life. Spirit guides from Heaven mentor the living. They provide pure simple guidance to situations in life.

CHAPTER 13

RELEASED

I stood watching the flames burning inside the gas fireplace. I cherished my quiet time where I could just be. I knew the next clients were already on their way. After glancing at the clock I realized they were running a little late. Their tardiness wasn't a problem. This was a blessing in disguise, allowing me more time to myself.

Earlier in the day, my patience was definitely tested. I was in the middle of a session with a grieving mother, when a car full of ladies arrived an hour early. The zealous early arrivals parked in the driveway calling and texting me from their cells. I chose to ignore the demanding rash of beeps and buzzes that followed each attempt. Shortly after the calls ended, the kitchen door flew open. A middle aged woman ran frantically up to the kitchen table. "We're here. You didn't answer your phone?" Her sweaty hands gripped the table edge, bracing herself as she caught her breath.

"Excuse me!" I snapped, looking at her as I rose to my feet. "You're interrupting my client's session." The mourning mother sat there in disbelief wiping away tears.

"You didn't answer your phone." The lady carried on. "We wanted to know, if we could see you now?"

"You're interrupting this lady's appointment. You must wait your turn." I spoke firmly as I walked towards the door to let her out.

"I'm sorry," she said "I thought you gals were just having coffee... and ignoring us." Guilt and shame quickly owned her crimson face. Without another word, she turned around, walked out the door and returned with her friends an hour later. The remainder of the day went smoothly…

The night sky was brightly lit by the glowing moon. I sat enjoying the comfort of my reclining chair by the burning fireplace. The flickering flames offered a different sense of relaxation, allowing me to unwind. It wouldn't be long before my last clients of the day arrived. The energy in the room suddenly shifted. I started to feel uneasy moments before a disturbing image flashed before my eyes. The vision revealed a couple driving down a freeway struggling to keep their car in gear. They were having difficulty with a stick shift in their car.

Before I realized the full extent of the situation, my left eye lid was flickering out of control. Intense pressure invaded my third eye. A crimson red blob appeared which kept darting erratically across the room. I instantly realized this angry entity was attached to the late couple. I picked up my phone and dialled the couple's cell phone hoping to reach them. The negative one interfered by disconnecting every call I attempted to make. This wayward spirit was desperately trying to keep everyone apart. A half-hour later the couple finally made it to the door.

"Hi Laura, we're Lynette and Lyle," the young couple introduced themselves. "You wouldn't believe what happened to us, Lynette piped up as she tugged at her sweater straightening it out.

"The one who haunts you has already paid me a visit," I mentioned this while leading them to the reading area. This evening was going to be challenging…no matter what…and I knew it. Tonight many unfavourable truths were going to be spoken. I needed to be in control of the situation at all times. I knew at anytime things could start flying. I silently asked for protection as we walked down the hall. The thought of what this spirit could be capable of doing was disturbing. I've seen a lot over the years, but this one was extremely powerful which was very concerning.

"Laura," Lyle confided, "I'm not a crazy man, but since my father passed my life has been horrible. A silhouette of a man keeps showing up and following me around. He seems rather harmless and shows up at random times in different places. This stalker ghost even rides with me in my truck. He's shown up at my workplace. I haven't told anyone else. I'm scared of being locked up and drugged for life." Lyle started squirming in his chair.

"What you're describing to me is your spirit guide." I explained.

"What the hell is that and what does it want?" He started getting uptight. "Is he causing me to be overwhelmed with evil thoughts?"

"Lyle, this is your spirit guide. He's here to help and protect you."

"Can you tell that presence to take a hike? My life is hard enough already. I don't need him screwing with my head." The young man fists were clenched tight on his lap.

"He's a mentor from Heaven and he's here to help you. This guide knows all about you and the lessons you're here to learn. Life is much easier if you allow him in. Consider yourself lucky, many people never have had the opportunity to physically see and work with their guides."

"Are you telling me he's an angel?"

"No, the angels are different. They protect us, but they do not guide us. They're more like the police in our time of need."

"That makes sense. I didn't see any wings on him. Do the angels have wings?"

"Yes most of the time, except when they appear in human form." I was pleased he was able to grasp things fast. I knew things were going to get ugly before the night was out. It was going to be a matter of time before the destructive one returned.

"Do you want to hear something weird? I started reading your first book, until I felt so disturbed that I couldn't finish it." Lyle started to explain. "Whoever is doing this, doesn't want me reading your story. It completely shredded all the pages between the covers."

"What do you mean?" My curiosity started kicking in. I've experienced a few of these dark entities in my time. These ferocious types are rare, but scary. They take great joy in destroying objects, and tormenting people. I can recall one burning a house to the ground.

"Whatever this is, it shredded your book and left the inside pages hanging from the book bindings like coleslaw, but the front and back cover remained completely untouched and intact. I started feeling badly about seeing you. I almost cancelled my appointment. The gear stick in the car stopped working – on the freeway! We tried calling you, but we were disconnected every time. The closer we got to your place, the harder it tried to steer us away from you. This thing is ruining my life. I've had terrible feelings that a person should never have. I feel like I'm turning into an evil person. Sometimes I feel like harming random strangers. I'm afraid that I'll kill someone if this isn't stopped. I'd do your ex-husband Derrick in a heartbeat. I was livid after reading what he put you through. Would you like him removed?" The evilest expression crossed his face as he waited for my answer.

"No thank you Lyle. He is dying. His days are numbered. He'll be gone when the grass is yellow and a slip of snow is on the ground. A couple of years ago one of my guides told me, 'she won't pay and he goes.' Obviously this is a volatile situation for him. I'm gathering his blood pressure spikes and brings on a heart attack or a stroke."

"Almost a year ago I was having my hair dyed at a salon," I continued. "While waiting for the colour to take the word DIE was spelled out in huge alphabetical blocks. This was followed by a movie like premonition. This showed him laying unconscious in a hospital bed hooked up to many machines. I've heard through the grapevine that he's a very sick man and on his last legs. Recently I've been shown him dropping dead with what appears to be either a heart attack or a massive stroke. His heart is black in other words dying and it quivers a couple of time. Suddenly I hear a loud thud as his two hundred fifty pound body hits the floor. A female's voice can be heard hollering No!" and crying hysterically in the background. He's rushed to the hospital by ambulance. He ends up on life support. I don't know how much time elapses, but the plug is pulled. A white sheet covers his head and the cord with the prongs is gently laid across his motionless chest."

"And if that bastard doesn't die?"

"He will. I've been shown different events leading to his last days. I trust my guides – they're never wrong. Sometimes my interpretation of the timing is can be off, but the events always happen – Lyle, let's get back to your issues." I shut my eyes and connected with his spirit guide. I was shown a dark entity attached below his left shoulder blade several layers into his aura, which is similar to the layers found in onions.

The entity was holding this man hostage. I felt this entity was latched onto him from a past life, but I need to quickly figure out why. Lyle wasn't possessed. He was being bullied and had no way of defending himself. I opened my eyes in the nick to time. A picture hanging on the wall spun in circles in its place, before being yanked off the wall and thrown to the floor by an invisible force. Shards of glass scattered around the floor. The war was on.

(This situation reminded me of a recent radio show where a huge picture fell to the floor the moment I entered the broadcast booth. The host started of his show by announcing these events. 'Now that Laura Laforce has finished wrecking our studio, perhaps she can sit down and talk with us and take a couple of calls from you listeners.' The station manger came frantically running in. "We're off the air. What's going on? We're off the air." The DJ's deceased grandfather had pulled a silly prank. Everything was totally restored within thirty seconds).

But *this* entity was different – it was seriously angry. Lynette jumped, letting out a shriek, as her purse strap that rested beside her feet slithered up her leg. Trying to control the situation, she picked up her purse and placed it on the empty chair beside her. A few seconds later, her purse was thrown about four feet from the chair. Most of the items from her purse were strewn along the floor. The leather purse landed upside down against the wall in a heap. The shocked couple sat speechless, holding each other's hands.

"Stop" I spoke with an authoritative voice. "Stop this now. These people are not to be touched. My house and anything within it is off limits. I am not to be messed with." I got up and started making my way towards Lyle. "God send in your angels and any available spirit guides. We need help. Please surround us and keep us safe." The dark entity attached to Lyle was pure evil. "Lynette let go of Lyle's hand and stay where you are. Lyle put your hands on your lap. You have an entity hidden in the layers of your aura from a past life."

"How do you know that?"

"Your guide has shown me. I need to work quickly. You two were enemies in a past life. You two killed each other. He's been controlling you by trying to destroy your life." In order to stop the activity Lyle's energy ties with the entity needed to be broken. "Lyle, tell him the contract is over. Tell him to go, your debt is paid, you owe him nothing." I stood behind Lyle and started working through the layers of his aura with my bare hands. My spirit guide was providing explicit visual guidance. All I had to do was follow with my hands exactly what I was shown. I started peeling back the layers of his aura's energy, which was behind his left shoulder blade. My energy started to shift to a strength I had never encountered before. I didn't have time to question this. I needed to keep going. Awhile later I reached the layer containing the root of this entity. A screaming blackened head without a body started emerging through the opening. I was guided by spirits and moved my hands to cup its head in both my hands, almost like delivering a baby. Removing the entity's core instantly cut the energy connection. My hands and body ached and trembled, as I released the entity with the help of my guide. "How are you feeling Lyle?"

"My head is spinning and my entire body is tingling."

"Don't worry," I reassured him, "that's normal with the amount of energy you've released. You'll be okay. You need to stay put for a few minutes." I was relieved this entity was lifted without too much hassle.

Lynette turned to me and asked: "Laura, can I ask you a couple questions? What do you see for me?" Lynette's energy looked rather grey. She arrived tonight wearing the aura of death. Her face looked distorted through the energy that draped her. *Oh my God... I can't save her,* I realized. I started to feel desperate. No wonder I had focused my attention away from her. It wasn't anything intentional.

"You end," fell out of my mouth before I could stop myself. We both looked at each other as tears welled in our eyes. "I'm sorry Lynette, I am so sorry. Is there anything I can do to for you?" By now tears were trickling down our faces. This was one of my worst moments; besides the time I told a mother her missing child was dead. Lyle sat speechless beside her, fighting back his tears.

Lynette wiped at her tears. "I have stage four cancer. I wanted to know if I left the country for treatment, if I could save my life. The doctors here are no longer treating me with chemo or radiation. I want to live. I've spent thousands traveling the world for a cure. Can that facility in Mexico extend my life?"

I was shown by my guide that she was in denial about the severity of her condition. Spirit I need an answer for her. I sat silently waiting and nothing happened.

"Lynette, you're dying. You've done everything you can. I can't answer your question. I haven't been given an answer. It is your choice to make." It took everything I had to keep myself together without breaking into tears.

"The doctors have told me I only have about six weeks to live. I was hoping for a different answer from you or the guides. Thank you for your honesty." Lynette started sobbing uncontrollably. Lyle and I tried consoling her. Two weeks later, I received a call from her mother telling me that Lynette died at six in the morning.

The following day I received a verbal message while sleeping. Everything was black. I couldn't see a thing. I could hear a child's voice telling me grandma's dead. I responded by telling her that's okay, she lived along life. No Mom, your mother's dead. The message was so intense that I awoke immediately. My ears rung for three weeks straight, because of the energy that accompanied it. In less than 6 months my mother was dead and I was numb.

A couple days later, I received a call from a nosey old neighbour. "Hi Laura, this is Liz, I used to live beside you in the white house. Do you remember me?"

"Yes"

"I just got word that your ex is dead. Derrick was extremely upset and had a massive heart attack yesterday. They pulled the plug this morning."

"What was he upset about?" I knew Liz was the neighbourhood gossip and would gladly spill the beans.

"Derrick's been sick and broke. The government was after him for more than twenty-five grand. The bank was threatening to foreclose on his house. The county was threatening to go after his house for unpaid property taxes. Remember Suzie, the cop's daughter he used to deal drugs with? He did a side job for her last week. Yesterday she refused to pay him..."

The death of my ex-husband, Derrick Stevenson, spelled relief for me. The deceptive maniac was finally dead. Derrick could never hurt me again. I was free from his abuse, stalking, attempts to kill me, property damage, high speed road chases, lies, and vengeful acts of manipulation including a variety of fraudulent events. No matter what he did to me, he always got away with it. There was always an out or a loophole for Derrick with the authorities.

Every life has a contract chalked full of lessons to be learned for spiritual growth. Old souls often reincarnate with complex issues and complicated lives. They are expected to grow through extreme challenges that wrap up the loose ends from past lives. People are often recycled in together to finish dealing with the unresolved issues from their previous lives.

In a past life, Derrick and I were enemies who fought for power and control. There had been a deadly battle on horseback, which I ended up galloping away from with a tied leather bound book in my hand. In this life time, we were married and he nearly destroyed me. He was obsessed with power and control. The stakes were costly and my losses were immense. Before Derrick's reign of terror was over, he deceptively manipulated my entire family, gradually luring them away one by one.

"Thank you Liz, it was nice hearing from you." I hung up the phone and rushed over to the window whipping open the drapes. The grass in the yard was yellow with traces of snow. A flood of relief washed over me. I no longer had to look over my shoulder. I was finally free.

About the Author

Laura Laforce

Every challenge offers a unique opportunity. Every encounter holds spiritual growth. Living with an open mind we become wiser.

You can learn how to open your third eye and receive messages from beyond the veil. Can you imagine being able to see a loved one who's passed on face to face.

Spirit guides lead us. Loved ones who've passed on are trying to contact us. Angels are speaking and revealing important messages.

Being gifted, I've spent my life learning how to work with my ability. My dream is to help people to access and utilize this divine connection, simplifying their lives

Love is the answer. Our souls are universal and capable of connecting, and Heaven is real.

.

X-TENDING

Manor House
905-648-2193
www.manor-house.biz